A

DEFENCE

OF

Mr. KENRICK's REVIEW

OF

Dr. JOHNSON's SHAKESPEARE:

BY
WILLIAM KENRICK

AMS PRESS
NEW YORK

A

DEFENCE

O F

Mr. KENRICK's REVIEW

O F

Dr. JOHNSON's SHAKESPEARE:

CONTAINING A NUMBER OF

CURIOUS AND LUDICROUS ANECDOTES

O F

LITERARY BIOGRAPHY.

BY A FRIEND.

LAUGH; for you *muſt* : be *candid*, if you *can*.   POPE.

L O N D O N,

Printed for S. BLADON, in Pater-noſter Row,

MDCCLXVI.

Library of Congress Cataloging in Publication Data

[Kenrick, William] 1725?-1779.
   A defence of Mr. Kenrick's Review of Dr. Johnson's
Shakespeare.

   1. Johnson, Samuel, 1709-1784. Johnson on Shakespeare. 2. Shakespeare, William, 1564-1616 — Criticism
and interpretation. I. A friend. II. Title.
PR2975.J653K4   1974   822.3'3   74-144646
ISBN 0-404-03658-9

Reprinted from the edition of 1766, London
First AMS edition published, 1974
Manufactured in the United States of America

AMS Press, Inc.
New York, N.Y. 10003

PREFACE.

THE formality with which this little performance is divided into sections, and illustrated with notes, may possibly give umbrage to the more sprightly and volatile criticks of the present times. This method, however, was chosen, left any confusion should arise in the minds of readers of little attention and short memories, from the writer's unnoticed transition from one thing to another, in treating of those various subjects, high and low, serious and comick, general and personal, which are contained in the following sheets.

By

80114

By this method, alſo, the convenience of thoſe perſons is ſuited, whoſe time may poſſibly be too precious to admit of their peruſing the whole, and yet may have an itching curioſity to look at ſome particular part.

C O N-

CONTENTS.

SECT.

CONTENTS.

SECT. VI.

Of the ingenuousness, impartiality, and urbanity of Sylvanus Urban, Gent. regarding the writings of Mr. K. and particularly his Review of Dr. Johnson's Shakespeare.

SECT. VII.

Remarks on the strictures of the Candid Reviewers, and the other volunteer criticks that have taken upon them to abuse the Reviewer of Dr. J's Shakespeare.

SECT. VIII.

On the modesty of men of letters.

SECT. IX.

On literary knowledge; with some remarks on IGNORANCE *and* INATTENTION.

POSTSCRIPT.

Addressed to the MONTHLY REVIEWERS.

A DE-

A

D E F E N C E

O F

Mr. KENRICK's REVIEW

O F

Dr. JOHNSON's SHAKESPEARE.

SECTION I.

INTRODUCTORY.

WHAT a well-bred age do we live in? Time was, when writers might boldly call in queſtion the abilities of each other, without incurring the cenſure of *malignity*, or even ſometimes forfeiting their title to diſtinguiſhed urbanity; when the meaneſt individual in the Republick of Letters had a right to bring the charge of *ignorance* or *inattention* againſt the proudeſt champion that ever brandiſhed gooſe-quill; when he might cite the accuſed to appear at the bar of the publick, and give teſtimony in plain terms againſt him without ceremony or equivocation. Time was, I ſay, when this impartial tribunal alſo, attentive only to the matter of fact and the evidence laid before it,

B

paffed fentence on the *convicted* without refpect of perfons, honouring the profecutor with its thanks and
protection, as a friend to juftice and the interefts of
literature.

How different is the cafe at prefent! when the fanc-
tion of a literary reputation, however obtained, is fimilar to the privilege of a feat in parliament, however
acquired; though it be notorious that ignorance and
partiality fometimes operate as powerfully in the one
cafe, as bribery and corruption in the other. But
when the returning officers have chaired the candidates,
and their opponents have not influence enough to get
them expelled the houfe, it is theirs to fit in judgment on their fellow fubjects, and give laws to the
world of letters.

It is well, however, for the progrefs of *Science*, and
the independency of *Wit*, that the Seffion of the Literary Junto is not fo firmly eftablifhed as that of parliament. They are both provided, indeed, with their
ufhers of the black rod, and their ferjeants at arms re-
fpectively; but, however tremendous may be the political authority of the one, nothing can be more ridiculous than the critical mock-majefty of the other.

The author of the Review of Dr. Johnfon's Shakefpeare hath, it feems, been committed to the cuftody
of thefe literary mirmidons, and formally proceeded
againft for a breach of privilege. The Doctor, we are
told, was above being called to account by any private
individual whatever; it being the higheft indignity to
the *majority* even to fufpect the inability of a writer,
whom they had been pleafed to vote *infallible*.

As

As a friend to the *Reviewer*, therefore, I take up the pen to defend his caufe, and affert the right of every citizen in the Republick of Letters, to think and write freely. To this I am particularly incited alfo, from a due fenfe that fuch freedom is become abfolutely neceffary to fupport the prefent interefts of literature; which are daily drooping under the dead weights of indolence, partiality, and prepoffeffion.

I am not infenfible that thefe obftacles to the progrefs of fcience, and the advancement of letters, are commonly called by other names. I well know that, in this age of civility and falfe refinement, mere COURTESY is termed *candour*, CEREMONY is called *politenefs*, QUAINTNESS *elegance*, PEDANTRY *erudition*, and DULLNESS *decency* and *decorum*. On the other hand, SINCERITY is termed *infult*, CENSURE is called *cruelty*, and WIT and HUMOUR *petulance* and *ill-manners*. In the mean time a zeal for *truth* is looked upon as a kind of canine madnefs; and a heart-felt veneration for true genius and learning is defpifed as a literary phrenzy. Thus are we degenerated from our forefathers; from the wits and philofophers of thofe ages which produced a Shakefpeare, a Bacon, a Dryden, and a Milton; whom inftead of imitating, we exert all our little abilities to depreciate, and level with the diminutive ftandard of the prefent times. A late noble writer obferves, refpecting our moral and political character, that we are now-a-days fo far from having the *virtues* of great men, that we have not even their *vices*; every thing, fays he, is little, mean, and pitiful among us. This might with greater juftice be faid of our

literary

literary character; our tafte for works of real genius, true fcience, and folid erudition, being almoft dwindled into nothing. In the mean time we fee the petty pretenders to wit and learning induftriously forming themfelves into parties for the fupport of each other, becaufe they find themfelves unable to ftand alone. Imbecillity naturally tends to render people complacent and civil; while the cunning, ufually attendant on ignorance, artfully teaches them to make a merit of their weaknefs, and to impute even their pufillanimity to candour and benevolence.

It is no wonder that a writer, who hath the fortitude alone to attack one of the greateft of thefe partial and illiberal combinations, fhould create himfelf a number of enemies; nor is it indeed a wonder that the impartial publick fhould, for a while, be mifled by the felf-interefted clamours, which fo numerous a body of partifans may raife againft him. It is boldly prefumed, however, that if the publick fhould fully and coolly enquire into the real ftate of the cafe, the motives for fuch attack, and the merits and demerits of the parties affailed and defended, they will not only acquit the Reviewer of the falfe charges of illiberality and malignity brought againft him; but will be ready to acknowledge that the chaftifement Dr. Johnfon hath received at his hands, is no lefs defenfible with regard to its feverity, than it is juftifiable in refpect to its caufe.

S E C T.   II.

Reasons for the Reviewer's having a less exalted opinion of Dr. J's abilities than has been entertained by the publick in general.

THERE is nothing which, at first fight, gives us greater offence or disgust, than to see those persons or characters, for whom we have been used to entertain a certain degree of respect, treated with familiarity or contempt. Nor is it at all necessary to this end, that such treatment should on their part be merited. It is enough that we are ignorant of their demerits ; of which it is afterwards very difficult to convince us, even by the strongest testimony. We are by no means easily reconciled to such an instance of our want of sagacity, as that of having long entertained a favourable opinion, much less a kind of reverence, for an object unworthy of it. We are apt to hesitate, therefore, at the most flagrant proofs of our mistake, and even to take offence at any supposed indignity offered to such characters, as if it in some measure affected ourselves.

This hath been remarkably the case in the present affair of Mr. K's Review of Dr. Johnson's Shakespeare ; even those, who could not fail of being convinced of the justice of the Reviewer's remarks, finding in themselves something repugnant to the ludicrous and farcastical manner in which Mr. K. had thought proper to reprehend this editor. Admitting for the present, however, that the cause of such reprehension was just, they

cannot

cannot fail, on reflection, to impute that repugnance to their prepoffeffion in favour of Dr. J. and their ignorance of the Reviewer's having ftill farther motives for his feverity, than appeared on the face of his pamphlet.

That none of thefe motives were perfonal, the Reviewer hath repeatedly and publickly declared. What they were, may be gathered from this and the following fections.

The Reviewer, it feems, had been fome years abroad, when he firft heard of the publication of Dr. Johnfon's Dictionary ; a work of which he had formed the higheft expectations from the fuppofed abilities and great reputation of its author. At the fame time, being apprehenfive that his own application to the ufe of foreign languages might, in fome meafure, corrupt that of his native tongue, he procured Dr. J's apparently elaborate performance, in order to correct both his memory and judgment, as either might occafionally fail him. Having thus, during an interval of feveral years, had more frequent occafions to confult an Englifh dictionary, than poffibly would have happened to him in any other fituation, he could not fail of being greatly furprized and difappointed at the many palpable and grofs miftakes which had efcaped this celebrated lexicographer. He was not fo unreafonable to expect, indeed, that, in a work of fuch extent, a number of trivial, and perhaps fome important errors, fhould not efcape the moft attentive and induftrious compiler. He could neither expect, however, nor overlook such an amazing number of blunders and inconfiftencies in etymology, orthoepy, idiom and grammatical conftruction, ſtruction, as were to be found in a work, which was boaſted of as a capital undertaking, and recommended to foreigners as a ſtandard of the Engliſh language.

He would have been careleſs of the honour, and wanting to the literature of his country *, had he not every where taken a proper occaſion, therefore, to ſpeak of the defects and imperfections of Dr. Johnſon's Dictionary. At the ſame time, that he might not be thought to depreciate the labours of another, without ſufficient cauſe, he amuſed himſelf occaſionally with forming a table of *errata* to that performance, intending ſome time or other to offer it to the proprietors; and, in caſe of their refuſal to accept it, to lay it before the publick.

The Reviewer's liſt of errors was pretty copious when he returned to England; ſince when, having applied more cloſely to literary matters, he hath increaſed it almoſt tenfold, and that by no means to the honour of Dr. Johnſon's boaſted erudition and profound knowledge of the Engliſh tongue.

This detection of the *Lexicographer* induced the Reviewer to make a cloſer examination, than he had before done, into the compoſitions of the *writer*; in which were found the ſame traces of *inattention* to the idiom of our tongue, and of his imperfect acquaintance with other modern languages. In the mean time, he

---

* Eſpecially as he obſerved that ſucceeding dictionary-writers, both abroad and at home, implicitly adopted the moſt egregious errors on the authority of Johnſon. Sufficient proof of this may be had by an examination of Bailey's Dictionary, improved by Scott; Baretti's Italian and Engliſh Dictionary, and others.

was found to be eternally aiming at the introduction of Latinifms, and other vicious modes of expreffion, by way of *enriching* our tongue ; but thereby corrupting it, as he himfelf fays of Shakefpeare, ' by almoft every ' mode of depravation.'

In his productions of imagination, his invention ap-peared weak and languid. It exerted itfelf, indeed, now and then with tolerable fuccefs in a *dream* or vi-fion ; but it was hardly ever wide awake, without feem-ing fatigued with its efforts toward vigility, and invo-luntarily dropping into a doze again. As to his works of knowledge and judgment, there appeared hardly any trace of the author's acquaintance with the fciences in any of his writings ; nay, even his pre-tended profundity in morals, and the knowledge of mankind, feemed to the Reviewer nothing more than a quaint and affected exhibition of the trite obferva-tions and hackney'd reflections of others.

His greateft merit appeared to confift in the labour thrown away on the tawdry glare of defcription, and the gloffy, but fading, polifh of ftile. Inftead of pro-ducing great and noble images, he feldom reached far-ther than high-founding words. Inftead of new and really elegant turns of thought, his novelty and refine-ment generally ended in fome florid allufion, quaint antithefis, or fantaftical precifenefs of expreffion. His verfe feemed heavy, cold and fpiritlefs ; and his profe alternately pompous and puerile.

A farther acquaintance with Dr. Johnfon's literary character, acquired even among and from his own friends,

friends, had by no means contributed to remove Mr. K's unfavourable opinion of this writer, when his long-expected edition of Shakefpeare made its appearance.

Having been already fo egregioufly difappointed as to the philological abilities of Dr. J. the Reviewer's expectations were by no means fo fanguine as before. His enthufiaftic veneration for Shakefpeare, however, could not be reftrained within the bounds of filence, on finding this editor had taken every opportunity to depreciate the merit of that incomparable bard ; on whom Dr. J. hath, in repeated inftances, (as is fhewn in Mr. K's Review) endeavoured to fix the charge of *incapacity*, *folly*, *vulgarity*, *immorality* and *impiety*.

To aggravate all this, Dr. J. falls with equal violence on the only commentator on Shakefpeare, that, by his own confeffion, hath acquitted himfelf with reputation ; charging him with *weaknefs*, *ignorance*, *meannefs*, *faithleffnefs*, *petulance* and *oftentation*.

Thofe who complain of Mr. K's feverity, and charge him with fcurrility, ill-manners and abufe, would do well to look through his work, and fee if they can find any paffage wherein he hath called Dr. J. *mean*, *faithlefs*, *immoral* or *impious*.

' But Shakefpeare and Theobald are *dead*, and Dr.
' Johnfon is *alive* ; the former cannot fuffer by any thing
' that is faid of them, whereas the latter may be effen-
' tially hurt by an attack on his reputation.' This may be urged, indeed, by thofe who conceive Mr. K's exceffive zeal for the honour of the dead is lefs excufable than Dr. J's excefs of tendernefs for the reputation of the living. It is very certain that, as they

C   arife

arife from different motives, they muft neceffarily inter-
fere with, or counteract each other. It is difficult,
indeed, to fay which favours moft of envy and malignity *. We may envy the reputation both of the living
and the dead ; but can hate only the living. Even hate,
however, may arife from laudable principles, as honeft
men deteft knaves, and lovers of truth abhor falfe-
hood : but envy, whether directed to the living or dead,
is a mean and odious paffion. At the fame time, it
muft be univerfally allowed more brave and honour-
able, though it may be lefs prudential, to attack the
reputation of the living than the dead. Now fortitude
hath ever been efteemed the general concomitant of
ingenuoufnefs and candour, which never harbour in
envious minds.

So far Mr. K. hath evidently the advantage over
Dr. J. Befides, the friends of the latter, while they
charge the former with envy at Dr. J's abilities and reputation, accufe him at the fame time with infufferable
felf-fufficiency and vanity. But if the contempt with
which he hath treated Dr. J. proceed really from his
vanity and felf-fufficiency, there is the lefs room to
think him fubject to the motives of envy ; for we never can envy thofe we truly defpife. The truth, I
imagine, is, that Mr. K. neither does the one nor the
other by Dr. J. notwithftanding he hath fufficiently
fhewn a fixed deteftation of that editor's literary mif-
conduct. This deteftation, as I obferved before, may
neverthelefs be very juft and laudable ; in which cafe

* It is very juftly obferved, however, by a late ingenious French
writer ; S'il eft horrible d'infulter aux vivans combien plus odieux
eft il de fletrir la reputation des morts !

its

its effects cannot, with any propriety, be imputed to malignity.

I fhould now proceed to enquire how far Dr. John-fon may be defended from the fufpicion of envy, as the motive for his abufe of Theobald and Shakef-peare.

As it behoves others, however, to exculpate the Doctor, I fhall only propofe a few queftions to thofe of his friends, who may chufe to anfwer them ; fuch anfwers, in my opinion, tending effectually either to clear or convict him of acting from invidious motives.

S E C T.   III.

Queftions offered to Dr. Johnfon's friends, refpecting fome curious anecdotes of the life and literary conduct of that gentleman.

IT hath been faid, with regard to Dr. W-rb-r-t-n, that he abundantly deferved the fcurrility and abufe, which it is pretended Mr. K. hath thrown upon him ; ' becaufe he was the firft author who introduced ' fuch foul language into controverfy, which he never ' failed to beftow on all his opponents when he dared. ' But with Dr. Johnfon the cafe is otherwife ; he never ' gave any public offence, nor even engaged in any ' controverfy.

Thofe who affirm all this, appear to know but very little of Dr. Johnfon ; nay, even to forget the fact for which he is arraigned. Did he give no public offence in the circumftances attending his edition of Shakef-

peare ?

peare ? Did he not engage in a controverfy with almoft all his commentators ; beftowing the worft of foul language on his opponents when he dared ; that is, on thofe who were *dead ?*

The following queries, however, take in a farther retrofpect of Dr. J's literary conduct ; the general tenour of which will be found to be tinctured with an invidious difpofition, that he was fond of indulging in actions, which his timidity was too great to permit him openly to avow.

1. Who encouraged LAUDER in his infamous attempt to charge the author of Paradife Loft with plagiarifm from Maffenius and others ; clapping him on the back while he hopped about the town, exclaiming againft that *axacrable vellain* John Milton ?

2. Who was the manager or editor of the Gentleman's Magazine at that time, and kept out the papers written againft *Lauder* for feveral months together ; for which he afterwards apologized, when the impofition became flagrant, and the accufer himfelf, with imparallel'd effrontery, confeffed the forgery ?

3. Who recommended fuch a modeft gentleman to the lords Chefterfield and Granville, who honoured him with their protection, and rewarded him with an annuity, till even Dr. J's intereft could not prevent his being ignominiously turned out of doors ?

4. Who

4. Who actually wrote *Lauder's* pamphlet againſt *Milton* ?

5. What ingenuous motive could poſſibly induce Dr. J. to join in ſuch an invidious attempt, to depreciate the merit of one of the greateſt poets England had to boaſt ?

6. Was it not becauſe Milton was, in his private character, a man of republican principles, and an enemy to ecclefiaſtical tyranny and arbitrary power ?

7. What motive could induce Dr. J. to endeavour, in his Rambler, to leſſen the poetical reputation of the late Mr. Pope, by laboured criticiſms on a few of the moſt admired paſſages in his writings, and on thoſe *only ?*

8. Who wrote the ſevere and carping criticiſms on the epitaphs of the ſame author ; firſt publiſhed in the *Vifitor*, and afterwards retailed in the Magazines ?

9. Who adviſed and aſſiſted the celebrated and ingenious Mrs. Lenox to an attack on the greateſt poet the world ever produced, and that in the moſt eſſential part of his poetical character, in her *Shakeſpeare illuſtrated ?*

10. Who wrote Dr. J's New Dictionary of the Engliſh language ?

11. Whether Dr. J. ever read the Dictionary he is ſuppoſed to have written ?

12. Whether the capital improvement, intended by that Dictionary, was not the collection of the

authorities

authorities for, and the illuſtrations of, the uſe of Engliſh words ?

13. Whether theſe authorities and illuſtrations do not in many hundred places contradict the meaning of the words, as given by the lexicographer ?

14. Whether the writer hath not almoſt always miſtaken the very meaning of words when he has departed from former dictionaries ?

15. Whether he hath not, in a conſiderable number of inſtances, given the words without any meaning at all ?

16. Who wrote the propoſals for publiſhing the laſt edition of Shakeſpeare, and who executed the work, and how ?

17. Whether indolence be an excuſe for not doing what a man hath publickly undertaken, and is well paid for ?

18. Whether it be not an inſult to the common ſenſe and common honeſty of mankind, to pretend that the private *virtue*, even of the moſt ingenious and learned individual upon earth, ſhould exempt him from correction, when he affects to be himſelf exempted from the faithful diſcharge of the common duties of his profeſſion or calling ?

19. Whether imbecility and indolence be really good-nature and benevolence ; and whether, in an age of leſs ceremony and greater ſincerity, the magiſterial ſupineneſs, affected by Dr. J. would not be frankly called *pride* and *idleneſs* ?

20. Whether, if the above queſtions cannot be an-
ſwered, to the honour of Dr. J. what right either
he or his friends have to complain of the ſeverity
of the chaſtiſement beſtowed on him * ?

* To this ſcore of queries I ſhall beg leave to add a dozen more,
merely literary, and ſome of them not altogether confined to Dr.
Johnſon's conduct, but extending to that of his friends, who
have been pleaſed to abuſe Mr. K. on this occaſion.

1. Whether the Drs. J. and H. have not been long in a ſecret
and partial combination to applaud the writings, and enhance the literary reputation of each other ?

2. Whether the Gentleman's Magazine hath not, for many
years paſt, been notoriouſly proſtituted to this purpoſe ?

3. Whether the Rambler and the Adventurer, in their journey
to the temple of Fame, were not obliged, like travellers
that had but one horſe between them, to ride and tie, from
month to month occaſionally ?

4. Whether Dr. H. did not, many years ago, oblige the Reviewer with a letter, containing a long and elaborate criti-
ciſm on one of his puerile performances ; profeſſing an high
opinion of Mr. K's natural genius, and offering his beſt ſervices in directing its cultivation ?

5. Whether Mr. K. ever ſaw Dr. H. or gave him any cauſe of
offence ſince that time ; or whether he hath not ever ſpoken
of him and his writings with due reſpect ; while, on the
other hand, Dr. H. hath taken more than one opportunity
of endeavouring to obſcure the little merit to which Mr. K.
may have occaſionally pretended ?

6. Whether Dr. H. could have any other motive than Mr. K's
differing from him in political and religious principles ; and
how far ſuch a motive is admiſſible in the republick of
letters ?

7. How many lines Dr. J. wrote in the *Traveller*, for the auk-
ward compliment paid him by its author in the Uni-
verſal Muſeum ; when he ſtiled him the *glory of the Engliſh
nation* ?

8. How many more he is to write in Mr. G's next poem, for
his ſcribbling *nonſenſe* on the cover of Mr. K's Review at
the coffee-houſes ; for his verſes in the St. James's Chronicle of December 14, and for the favour he does the Reviewer in running about the town to abuſe him?

9. Whe-

S E C T. IV.

Whether Dr. J. deserves better treatment than he has received; and how far Mr. K. is excusable in having so treated him.

D R. Johnson's friends will doubtless object, that it is much easier to ask questions than to answer them, and that injurious inuendoes may be safely conveyed in the way of query, even though they should be groundless.

I should not have presumed to ask those questions, however, had not Mr. K. furnished me with authenticated materials for making a satisfactory reply to every single article, if the Doctor, or his friends, should at any time require it. It was thought proper, in the mean time, to state the merits of Dr. J's literary character rather in a problematical than a

9. Whether Mr. G. who rails at all Reviewers, was not himself a Literary Reviewer, till he was discarded for incapacity?

10. Whether Dr. J. himself did not make several efforts to assume a kind of dictatorship over a certain periodical Review, interfering on subjects, of which he was consummately ignorant?

11. Whether Mr. G. is not one of Dr. J's light-troops? and whether he does not harbour some resentment against Mr. K. for exposing his ignorance, when he [Mr. G.] took upon him to give an account of *The present State of polite Letters in Europe,* without even knowing the names of the celebrated writers now living on the continent?

12. How Mr. K. can fail to hold such invidious pretenders to exclusive knowledge in some degree of contempt, and, like a man of spirit, *openly* to treat them accordingly?

peremp-

peremptory manner, that his partizans might folve any difficulties that might arife, in the beft manner they are able. But if they cannot obviate fuch difficulties, and that very foon, it is not to be doubted that the good fenfe and impartiality of the publick will prevail over its former prepoffeffions, and determine for me that Dr. J. hath met with no worfe treatment than he deferves.

How far Mr. K. is defenfible in having inflicted it, is another matter of confideration. If the Reviewer, in the height of his zeal for the honour of Shakefpeare, hath given too great a loofe to his paffions, and hath expreffed himfelf unbecoming a fcholar and a gentleman, he hath in fo doing injured his own reputation more than he hath done that of Dr. Johnfon. Nor is it any juftification of Mr. K's fcurrility to fay it is a degree lefs fcurrilous than that of the Doctors J——n or W————n.

If their fault, however, be no juftification of his, it is fome excufe for the latter that it appears to be the natural effect of a refentment excited by nobler and lefs interefted motives.

To attack a man, in the warmth of refentment, however rudely, who is alive and able to defend himfelf, is certainly lefs exceptionable, in point of honour and fpirit at leaft, than a premeditated defign, conceived and executed in cold blood, to ftrip the dead of thofe honours which fucceffive ages had beftowed on their memory.

D   It

It is to be obferved alfo, that it is not very eafy for men of warm paffions, when affected with their fubject, to exprefs their refentment in terms always confiftent with the common forms of politenefs. Experience fufficiently evinces this, as we may be convinced by turning to almoft any polemic writings, even on thofe fubjects which in a peculiar manner require the appearance at leaft of the higheft degree of temper and benevolence.

There is one cireumftance, indeed, in which the Reviewer feems juftly to have incurred the cenfure of impolitenefs and want of urbanity. This is the reflection he hath made on a certain *natural* infirmity of Dr. J. In anfwer to this charge, however, it is to be obferved, that Mr. K. being perfonally a ftranger to the Doctor, and having formed the ideas of his character purely on the reprefentations of the Doctor's friends, he really miftook that infirmity for an affected habit ; as thofe very friends, in repeating Dr. J's bons mots, conftantly made ufe of the fame habit or infirmity to heighten the joke ; and therefore may be as juftly faid to have ridiculed it themfelves, as it is pretended Mr. K. has done. Nay, the Doctor's acquaintance are ftill more inexcufable, as they muft be fuppofed to have known the real ftate of the cafe, and ought not to have given occafion for fuch a miftake, in a writer who is mafter of fufficient acrimony of ftile, without defcending to ridicule perfonal defects, which he never could conceive to be ridiculous.

Having

Having now done with Dr. Johnson's demerits, as well as the merits of Mr. K's Review, with regard to its feverity in general, I shall proceed to take some notice of the principal objections that have been made to it by particular writers, especially by the authors of the Critical Review, the editor of the Gentleman's Magazine, the Candid Reviewers, and some few other volunteer criticks.

To begin with the first-mentioned, whose incon-confistent behaviour with regard to Mr. K's writings, even from the very commencement of their Review, may serve to elucidate their pretensions to impartiality, as well as their capacity to fit in judgment on works of genius or learning.

S E C T. V.

Specimens of the literary abilities and candour of the Critical Reviewers, occasionally exercised on the writings of Mr. K. and particularly on his Review of Dr. J's Shakespeare.

THE very ingenious and ingenuous authors of the Critical Review, having had frequent occasion to exercise their critical talents on the writings of Mr. K. it may not be amiss to take a retrospect of their former opinion of this writer's genius and abilities ; as it may serve, in some measure, to account for that which they affect to entertain at present.

When

When an imperfect edition of *Epiſtles to Lorenzo*
firſt made its appearance in England, theſe criticks,
who had not long before entered on their judicial of-
fice, approved of them as ſpirited, juſt, poetical, de-
ſcriptive, ſenſible and true *.

In their Review of the ſecond edition, they again
confeſſed ' they could not help admiring the perſpi-
' cuity, the ſpirit, the variety of the author's expreſſion
' and imagery † ;' concluding their ſtrictures with ſay-
' ing, We will candidly own our admiration of his
' genius, both as a poet and metaphyſician §.'

In ſpeaking of the ſame writer's tranſlations, they
expreſs themſelves with equal warmth of approbation.
—Of that of *Rouſſeau*'s *Eloiſa*, they ſay, ' It is but ju-
' ſtice to add, that we never peruſed a more ſpirited,
' juſt and elegant tranſlation than that of Eloiſa, though
' one of the moſt difficult performances in the French
' language, as it abounds with turns, ſentiments and
' idiomatical expreſſions, which will hardly bear being
' tranſlated into a foreign tongue ‡.'

Of *Geſner's Rural Poems*, they affirm, ' that in the
' harmony of the periods, the conciſeneſs, the elegance
' and ſimplicity of ſtile, the original German is hap-
' pily imitated by the Engliſh verſion.'

Will it be believed, when I affirm it, that theſe ju-
dicious criticks have, at other times, compared this

* CRITICAL REVIEW, vol. iii. page 164.
† Ibid, vol. vi. page 444.
§ Ibid, vol. vi. page 453.
‡ Ibid, vol. xii. page 211.

their

their admirable genius to Sternhold and Hopkins? or that, in their prefent ftrictures, they have charged fo fenfible, fo poetical, fo metaphyfical a writer, with having publifhed paultry obfervations, and ridiculous abfurdities, in his Review of Dr. Johnfon's Shakefpeare? Nay, fo treacheroufly has their fpleen dealt with their memory, that they have even ventured to pronounce that ' the Trevoux Dictionary appears to be the ne ' plus ultra of the French learning' of the author of the *fpirited, juft* and *elegant* tranflation of Eloifa!

The reader will very naturally afk, what can poffi-bly be the meaning of fuch ftrange inconfiftency?— I will endeavour to inform him. When the Critical Reviewers were fo lavifh of their encomiums on Mr. K's writings, they were either ignorant of his private connections, or that he was the author of fuch writings; and thus may be fuppofed to have fpoken of them to the beft of their judgment, without partiality or preju-dice. Mr. K. however, had no fooner fhewn himfelf above being elated with the applaufe of ignorance, and had corrected them for the fallacy of their hypercriti-cifms *, than they became immediately his enemies; and that in a more virulent manner, when he was known to give the preference to a rival Review. Such, it is prefumed, are the fecret fprings by which thefe tre-mendous judges of literary merit muft, in this cafe, appear to be actuated.

* In the *Scrutiny*, or the *Critics Criticifed*; for an account of which, fee the Critical and Monthly Reviews for the year 1759.

In

In support of this presumption, we shall here reca-
pitulate a few of those criticisms, on which they have
ventured to rest the merits of their censure.

" This Drawcansir of a Reviewer opens his work with a
specimen of his critical abilities, by correcting the following
passage in the Tempest, vol. i. p. 8.

PROS. to MIR. ' I have with such provision in mine art
So safely order'd that there is no SOUL :
No, not so much perdition as an hair
Betid to any creature in the vessel, &c.'

" Though we admit that Warburton's, Theobald's, and
Johnson's remarks on this passage are all absurd ; yet, we
think, our Reviewer has been ingenious enough to excel
them even in absurdity ; for he reads, instead of ' there is no
SOUL,' ' there is no ILL.' We will venture to say, that
there is no man of plain sense in the kingdom, who could
suspect a depraved reading in this passage, as it stood origi-
nally. Shakespeare says neither more or less, than that

——— ' there is no soul — viz. *perdition* ———
Nay, not so much perdition as an hair,
Betid to any creature, &c.

Well may Mr. Kenrick adopt the clench of ILL-BETIDE
such commentators."

Was ever poor devil so caught in the cob-web of
his own devices, as this unhappy *Critical* Reviewer ?
In the name of common sense what can he mean ? For
my part, I cannot even guess, so shall leave this saga-
cious criticism for the reader to explain as he can : ob-
serving only, in justice to Mr. K. that he proposes his
alteration only, in case of the supposed necessity of
making

making any alteration at all ; which he does by no means affirm. Again,

"ARIEL. ' Not a foul
But felt a fever of the mad, and plaid
Some tricks of defperation :'

" Mr. Kenrick is for fubftituting *a fever of the mind*. Mr. Johnfon is undoubtedly right in reftoring the old reading. Admitting it not to be quite idiomatical, yet it is poffeffed of ftrength fufficient to maintain its place againft mere conjecture. *Ex uno difce omnes*. The reft of his review of this play is of a piece with the fpecimens here exhibited."

Here the Critical Reviewer's ipfe dixit gives the preference to Dr. Johnfon's reading ; but the misfortune is, that what thefe Cricks impute to Mr. K. is the reading of all the modern editions, and not Mr. Kenrick's * ; fo that the reader hath here a moft notable inftance of their judgment and impartiality in exhibiting the above two criticifms as juft fpecimens of Mr. K's Review.

They proceed, neverthelefs, in the fame magifterial and dogmatical ftile to expofe their own ignorance ftill farther in the following paffages. His, fay they, that is, Mr. K's, " deriving the word *feodary* from the word *foedus*, a covenant, is an inftance of ignorance hardly to be paralleled. The beft Englifh writers fay *feodum*, inftead of *feudum*. A feodary therefore is one who owes fuit and fer-

---

* The editor of the Gentleman's Magazine, quoting this paffage from Mr. K's Review, fays, he would have it to be " *The* fever of the mad." An egregious proof this of the attention and capacity of thefe writers to correct Mr. K. who in fact only oppofes Dr. Johnfon's reading in this paffage ; advancing nothing of his own, except by way of mere hypothofis.

vice to his fuperior. Warburton's inaccuracy in fpell-
ing the word *feuda*, which is the Scottifh term, inftead
of *feoda*, has brought our Critick into a blunder. A feodary is no other than a *fervant*, an *agent*; and the very inftance brought by this Reviewer from Cymbeline confirms
it."

The word, whofe derivation is here difputed, is,
in fome editions of Shakefpeare, fpelt *fedary*, without
the dipthong. Suppofing Mr. K. to be miftaken,
however, which I do not believe to be the cafe, this
inftance of ignorance, as the critic calls it, is yet to be
parallel'd, as he may fee, by turning to Bailey's Dictionary, corrected and enlarged by Scot; where he
will find the fenfe of the word, and even of the paffage
quoted from Cymbeline, laid down in the fame manner.
Feuda may, for ought I know, be a Scottifh term,
and it may in Scotland mean a flave or fervant; but
neither Shakefpeare nor Mr. K. wrote Scotch, but
Englifh; of which it is hardly poffible for a Scotchman
ever to be a *compleat* mafter.

The next offence thefe criticks take at Mr. K's il-
luftration is his philofophical explanation of the word
warps in the famous fong of *Blow thou winter's wind*.
On which occafion they exprefs themfelves as follows:

"What a pity it is that this writer's whole difplay of critical and natural knowledge fhould be entirely thrown away;
fince nothing is more certain, than that Shakefpeare meant
no more by *warping*, but *fixing* or *freezing* the waters. The
allufion is drawn from the operation of weavers, who *warp*,
that is, *fix* their worfted or yarn in their looms before they
work it."

But,

But, how is it certain that Shakefpeare meant *no more but* fixing or *freezing*; when there is no proof that he meant even that : for, unlefs thefe criticks can produce the teftimony of one Englifh writer, or even one Englifh *weaver*, to prove that the term *warp*, as related to the *woof*, is ufed as a verb, nobody can give into their notion of the allufion.

The following obfervation affords a remarkable inftance of the modefty and learning of thefe critical gentry :

— " After all Mr. Kenrick's exultations at the difcovery of the meaning of the word *l'envoy*, in *Love's Labour loft*, his etymology is but fantaftical ; nor is it juftified by the Trevoux Dictionary, which feems to be the *ne plus ultra* of his French learning."

Indeed ! — In the firft place, Mr. Critick, you tell a notorious untruth in afferting a thing you know nothing of : you have looked, I fuppofe, into the *Dictionaire de Trevoux*, and becaufe you cannot find fuch etymology juftified by that work, you flatly affirm it to be fantaftical, and very logically conclude that, becaufe one Reviewer's French learning extends no farther than the Trevoux Dictionary, another's muft be confined to the fame limits. It appears, however, that Mr. K. has at leaft one dictionary more of French learning, as you call it, than you ; for I find in one, that he put not long fince into my hands, that his etymology of the word *envoy* is there juftified in the following words :

ENVOI. —— C'eft comme l'abregé du chant Roial, ou de la balade. Ce n'eft ordinairement

E que

que la moitié d'un couplet du chant Roial, ou de
la balade, qu'on fait à la fin des couplets de ces
fortes de poemes, & qui a été nommé *envoi*, parce
qu'on l'adreſſoit au prince des jeux floraux, pour
fe le rendre favorable dans la diſtribution des
prix. [L'envoi doit être delicat et ingenieux.]
DICTIONAIRE FRANCOIS, par P. Richelet,
a Geneve; chez Widerhold, 1680.

I ſhall mention but one more of their criticiſms ; as
it contains either a proof of their ſaying only what
other writers have ſaid before them, or of their rea-
dineſs occaſionally to adopt the ſagacity of others in
ſilence.

" We ſhall give him credit for his retaining the word *knot*
in the fame play ; but we ſee no authority he has for ſuppo-
fing the king to be a wounded knot, or bird, ſo called.
When we reflect, that he ſteps aſide and conceals himſelf
in a buſh, while he diſcovers the lovers, ſo as to be as invifible as a *gnat*, the badneſs of the rhimes is removed by
reading *gnat* inſtead of *knot* ; but this is mere conjecture.

It is really very good of theſe gentlemen to give ſuch
a *paultry obſerver* as Mr. K. credit for any thing ; eſpecially as they had nothing better to offer than mere
conjecture. But the worſt on it is, that this conjecture
was long ago conjectured by Mr. Pope, who adopted
the fame reading for the ſake of the rhime. This,
however, it is poſſible theſe criticks on the critick of
the editors of Shakeſpeare knew nothing at all about.

I come now to the more ſerious part of the offence,
which theſe criticks have both taken and given, with
regard to Mr. K's performance. This is the paſſage
immediately ſucceeding the above ; in which, admitting

3 that

that Dr. J's note is a *vile* one, they proceed to infinuate that Mr. K. in his reprehenſion of it, hath forfeited his pretenſions to *honour*, *ſpirit* and *virtue*. Nay, reader, don't laugh; it is really the *Critical* Reviewers, who, in this very article, " have entered their caveat againſt *illiberal* criticifm," and talk about *honour* and *virtue*; even thoſe, whoſe criticifm hath heretofore been deemed l——s, and as ſuch puniſhed accordingly. You will ſay, perhaps, that they are reformed; that they have ſince authorized their printer to pay fifty pounds, out of his own pocket, to any perſon who can bring legal proof of their having taken money for the inſertion of partial charaɛters of books and authors, although they own it has been offered them *. What an inſtance this laſt of their integrity, impartiality and *virtue*!—Very true, indeed, and I firmly believe that they never did take any pecuniary bribe on this account; for, though I am acquainted with many mercenary bookſellers, and as many vain authors, yet I don't know one, whom I think fool enough to value the beſt charaɛter they could give of his performance at three farthings. I will not contradiɛt them poſitively indeed, and ſay that not one ſuch is to be found; but

---

* See their late advertiſement inſerted in the news-papers, as alſo on the cover of the Critical Review, wiſely to inform the country reader of the high eſteem in which the Reviewers were held in town. It is well for them, indeed, that their rage of juſtification did not induce them to promiſe a reward for proving the editor guilty of receiving and inſerting anonymous articles, which might, for ought he knew, be written by the authors of the books themſelves : becauſe, in this caſe, there might have been brought ſuch damning proof, as might have made them tremble for the offered premium.

it

it happens extremely unlucky that thefe criticks, in thinking to do themfelves honour, fhould confefs a thing that cannot fail to entail on them difgrace. They own that money hath been offered them, though they had fo much *virtue* as to refufe to take it. Does not this circumftance alone fufficiently evince what opinion the perfons, offering the bribe, muft have of thofe to whom it was offered? — Oh! fie! fie! for fhame! never make this confeffion again, whether true or falfe, as you value your very exiftence. *Virtus poft mortem* may ferve well enough for a motto to the atchievement of a dead cheefemonger; but the virtue even of a Critical Reviewer is not worth a groat to an author, who is damned while he is alive.

For decency's fake be a little confiftent; and, for the future, beware of extolling the works of ftrangers to the fkies, and of endeavouring afterwards to drag them down again, when you find fuch writers know too much to be vain of your praifes, and are too fincere to become your friends. In vain may your hodmandod * of a printer difplay his brawny mufcles, and threaten to avenge your caufe by his fkill in the athletic fciences. You have yourfelves given Mr. K. the apellation of a Tartar; and can you imagine he is to intimidated by the frowns of a Saracen's head? Let not

---

* So called from a certain copy of verfes, handed about lately in manufcript, and intended to be printed — and thereby hangs a tale. The verfes, it feems, were tolerable good verfes; but the printer of the Critical Review, having a moft exquifite tafte for poetry, did not like them. The reader will judge for himfelf; they ran thus.

LUSUS

your difcreet hearts think it. Are there not ways and
means to curb the infolence of ruffians, and guard

LUSUS NATURÆ, TYPOGRAPHUS.

*I have thought that Nature's journeymen had made men, and not made
them well, they imitated humanity fo abominably.* Shakespeare.

In Nature's work-fhop, on a day,
Her *journeymen*, inclin'd to play,
　Half-drunk, 'twixt cup and can,
Took up a clod, which fhe with care
Was modelling a huge fea-bear,
　And fwore they'd make't a man.

They try'd, but handling ill their tools
Form'd, like a pack of bungling fools,
　A thing fo grofs and odd ;
That, when it roll'd about the difh,
They knew not if 'twas flefh or fifh,
　A man or hodmandod !

Yet, to compleat the piece of fun,
They chriften'd it *Arch* H————n. ————
　" *But what can this thing do?* ————
" Kick it down ftairs ; the devil's in't
" If it won't ferve to write and print
　" The C————l Review."

But to the ftory, Thefe verfes, as I faid before, would have appeared in the news-papers, had not the editors been either afraid
of the Caliban's refentment, or fearful of fetting a bad example to
authors; whom they would readily affift to maul any private gentleman, yea, a prince of the blood-royal, if he were dead and
nailed in his coffin, but not to barbacue a live printer. By refufing
to infert them, however, they robbed the publick of an egregious
entertainment ; for it can hardly be doubted that the lovers of tur-
tle, whom Mr. H. lately treated at a guinea a head, would be
equally fond of the calipafh of a roafted hodmandod.

To proceed, however, in my tale ; the poornefs of the verfifi-
cation was not the only fault that was found with the above ftan-
zas. Mr. H———— infifted on it they were actionable at law,
and therefore proceeded gravely to lay the following queries before
council.

Query 1. Whether it be not actionable at law for a poet to call
　　a printer a hodmandod ?

2. If

againſt the malice of aſſaſſins ? Have we not Hyren
here ! Farewel — be adviſed and proſper.

S E C T. VI.

Of the ingenuouſneſs, impartiality, and urbanity of Syl-
vanus Urban, Gent. regarding the writings of Mr. K.
and particularly his Review of Dr. Johnſon's Shake-
ſpeare.

EVE RY body knows who was the original Sylvanus Urban, honeſt Cave, who, little as he knew of literature or ſcience himſelf, had yet ſo much knowledge
and diſcretion as to ſet a juſt value on his friends and
correſpondents, and behave to them at leaſt with gra-
titude and common decency. When the neceſſity, indeed, of employing perſons of ſuperior genius and
learning obliged him to lean on ſome right-hand-man,
he could not always be accountable for what he was
urged to do by others. In time Sylvanus Urban be-

2. If ſo, what method is moſt adviſable for the plaintiff
to proceed in order to recover damages ; and what
damages a Middleſex jury might be reaſonably ſuppoſed to give ?

The anſwer to the above queries, as I am informed, were to the
following purpoſe. " An action on the caſe will undoubtedly lie.
—Fact proved ; damages high, proviſo plaintiff proves hodmandod a fiſh of prey, as the ſword-fiſh, the ſhark, or the like. Lord
chancellor Bacon mentions it together with the tortoiſe : if the
jury take it to be an eatable fiſh, damages not ſo high, unleſs
not to be conveyed by land-carriage. Adviſes conſulting with
the naturaliſts ; above all, to admit the truth of the libel ; the
truth, in law, aggravating the offence.

came

came a mere fhadow ; and the good-will of his friends
was liable to be perverted by the caprice, ignorance,
or ill-will of his journeymen-editors. How far the
prefent Sylvanus is his own friend, in admitting of fuch
a perverfion, time hath already evinced in fome degree,
and will daily exhibit more plainly. Before I proceed
any farther, however, I fhall infert Mr. Urban's account of Mr. K's Review.

" This piece is written with a malignity for which it is
very difficult to account, as the authour declares that he is a
ftranger to Dr. Johnfon, and never received any offence from
him. If his ill-will arifes from envy of the literary honour
Dr. Johnfon has acquired, or the mark of diftinction he has
received from his fovereign, he is too much an object of pity
to move any other paffion in the breaft either of Dr. Johnfon,
or his friends *. He has treated the bifhop of Gloucefter with
the fame acrimony that he has treated Dr. Johnfon, yet he
declares he has himfelf fome literary reputation which he
would not wantonly hazard, being the author of two tranfla-
tions from the French, befides feveral anonymous pieces,
which, he fays himfelf, are too numerous to be good †.

* If the writer of this paragraph fufpects Mr. K. of the above-
mentioned motives from any thing his own heart fuggefts to him,
he is himfelf too much, and too mean a wretch to *deferve* pity.
And that he could have any other grounds, on which to form fuch
a fufpicion, he is called upon to make appear.

† Is this true ? — Is this a fpecimen of Mr. Urban's ingenuoufnefs, impartiality and veracity ? The truth is, that Mr. K. in the
Preface to his Review, fpeaking of his not ftanding exactly in the
fame predicament with the author of the Canons of Criticifm, who
had never written any thing before that piece, thought it neceffary
to add the following note, which the reader will fee Mr. Urban
has not only mutilated and mifreprefented, but hath given it the
moft invidious turn.

" In confirmation of what is here afferted, it may poffibly be
" thought neceffary to name fome of thofe publications, on which
" the

This work confifts principally of feveral conjectures‡, which he has fubftituted for the conjectures of the Bifhop and Dr. Johnfon, frequently with as much confidence as if they were truths received by revelation, and confirmed by miracle §; of thefe we fhall give fuch a fpecimen as will

"the public have conferred the honour of a favourable reception.—
"It is prefumed needlefs, however, to particularize performances
"that would certainly have been lefs faulty, had they been lefs nu-
"merous. The author contents himfelf, therefore, with men-
"tioning only his Epiftles to Lorenzo *; and the Tranflation of
"Rouffeau's Eloifa and Emilius."

‡ This is notorioufly falfe; Mr. K. having propofed very few conjectures; his work confifting principally of rational illuftrations of the poet, or proofs pofitive of the ignorance of his commentators.

§ Well, and what then? Why may not a writer fpeak confidently when he is convinced he is in the right? And I don't find that either Mr. Urban, or any other of Dr. Johnfon's friends, will venture to go about to prove Mr. K. in the wrong. They may rail in general terms; but if they meddle with particulars, they will poffibly only expofe their own nakednefs, and be laughed at with the Critical Reviewers.—But Mr. K. fpeaks, fays this *magaziner*, as if his criticifms were truths "received by revelation, and "confirmed by miracle." If he received them by revelation, however, I prefume there was no manner of occafion for his having them confirmed by miracle, to warrant his confidence. Their production was, neverthelefs, fo far miraculous, that they were written in fewer days than Dr. Johnfon took years to compleat his work: a circumftance which fome wifeacres, who never faw them, urged publickly, as a proof they could be good for nothing; becaufe,

* Can any thing be more pitiful and mean than the omiffion of the name of this work, with a view to reprefent Mr. K. as a mere tranflator? It is alfo foolifh as mean, for how long did this *ingenuus* critick think this expedient would ferve him? Did he think, becaufe when Mr. K. was an anonymous writer, he defpifed thefe little artifices too much to take notice of them, that when he had by name attacked their *chief*, he would not take an opportunity to crufh his pitiful dependents? Or did they imagine that, if Mr. K. fhould think them beneath his refentment, he would find none to join him in fo good a caufe? Could they conceive there was nobody who, while he was roafting the coloffus like an over-grown turkey-cock, for the entertainment of the publick, would take the trouble to fpit a dozen or two of his emiffaries, by way of larks, to garnifh the difh withal?——This critick was miftaken every way.——

faid

enable the reader to judge of the reft, beginning where the author begins, that our impartiality may not be brought into queftion."

Would not any indifferent perfons, who fhould read the above paffage, imagine at leaft that the writer of it never once heard of the Reviewer, or his writings, in his life? But are not Dr. H——h and Mr. H——y the editors and managers of the Gentleman's Magazine? And is it poffible that neither of thefe gentlemen remember that Mr. K. hath been an occafional contributor to their work from a very fchool-boy? And is this a fpecimen of the manners with which they treat a correfpondent, for whom they have more than once expreffed the higheft regard; and for whofe *valuable contributions* (as they have called them) they have even offered pecuniary gratifications, which he never condefcended to accept? I have now in my hands fufficient proofs of what is here intimated, and the Gentleman's Magazine affords various others of the *acknowledged* value of the papers Mr. K. hath fent it, refpecting very different branches of fcience and literature.

Can the managers of that work be fo mean and felf-interefted, as to treat Mr. K. in this fcandalous manner, becaufe he has of late years been induced to favour other periodical works of the like kind? They can have no other motive, unlefs it be their clofer attachment to Dr. J. But, however they may have been

---

faid they, " a man of moderate genius could not read the book in " the time that Mr. K. *ftans pede in uno* had produced a confutation " of it." But while the juftice of Mr. K's criticifms in general remain inconteftible, I leave the publick to judge, whether the rapidity of their compofition redounds moft to his credit or his difhonour.

F　　　　　　　obliged

obliged to that gentleman, and whatever opinion they may have of his literary abilities, are candour, truth and juſtice, all to give way to their partiality for him? Are the talents and reputations of the Doctors Johnſon and H———h ſo very bulky, that thoſe both of the dead and the living muſt be mangled, mutilated and depreſſed, in order to allow them room enough to vapour in? Surely the recent loſs of a *Lloyd* and a *Churchill* might have rendered them a *little* more at eaſe in ſo wide a world! But, no. They are determined to have the univerſe to themſelves and their partizans; condemning every one to defamation or obſcurity, who does not enliſt under the banner of the coloſſus *.

* Among numerous inſtances that might be brought of Mr. Urban's miſbehaviour in this kind to Mr. K. I ſhall only mention two or three; which, though beneath his own notice, may ſerve as a ſpecimen of thoſe *little arts*, by which ſome modern writers have wriggled themſelves into fame, and endeavoured to obſcure the dawning reputation of others. It is remarkable that the editor of the Gentleman's Magazine hath of late years carefully avoided mentioning the very name of Mr. K. though formerly pleaſed to print it in large capitals to a puerile and inſignificant performance, inſerted ſo long ago as the year 1748.——He hath been as cautious alſo of mentioning the *Epiſtles to Lorenzo*, a work of eſtabliſhed credit, not only in the pitiful inſtance before-given, but even in his liſt of books at the time of its publication.——When he thought proper alſo lately to reprint the fable, entitled, *Reaſon and Imagination*, (written by the CELEBRATED Mr. *Chriſtopher Smart*, as he himſelf ſtiles that gentleman) and addreſſed to Mr. K. he judged it expedient even to mutilate that piece, in order to omit the addreſs, as well as the following elegant compliment which is paid to Mr. K. at the concluſion.

> O, *Kenrick!* happy in the view,
> Of *Reaſon* and of *Fancy* too,
> Who reconcil'ſt with *Euclid's* ſcheme
> The tow'ring flight and golden dream,
> With thoughts at once *reſtrain'd* and *free:*
> I dedicate this tale to thee.

At

I

They are here given to know, however, that Mr. K. detefts all combinations in literature, as much as he defpifes the monopolifts of fame. Let thofe, who find themfelves unable to ftand alone, combine to fup-port each other. Mr. K. will go hand in hand with any fair and open enquirer after literary or fcientific improvement : but he is neither fo young and weak as to need the help of leading-ftrings, nor fo old and feeble as to require the affiftance of crutches. But to proceed.

Mr. Urban pretends, even after thus throwing out the moft infamous and groundlefs infinuations con-cerning the motives for Mr. K's Review, to feleft fuch a fpecimen of it, as may enable the reader to judge of the reft, without calling his impartiality in queftion. What thefe fpecimens are, may be feen at the bottom of the page * ; and how far they will juftify his impar-

At another time this editor promifed his readers an abftraft of what he called a *very fenfible* anonymous pamphlet, written by Mr. K. but, having learned the name of the author before the next month's magazine appeared, he fomehow forgot his promife, and poffibly has not recollefted it to this day. And yet, during all this time, not the flighteft occafion was neglefted in which Mr. Urban could compliment Dr. Johnfon or Dr. Hawkfworth. But I fear my readers are fufficiently difgufted at the recapitulation of fuch minute and pitiful artifices, which are as difgraceful to the profeffion of letters in general, as to thofe who practife them in particular.

I fhould otherwife mention fome more ferious and impor-tant caufes of complaint, proceeding obvioufly from the fame fource, which Mr. K. hath farther to exhibit againft the editor and manager of this magazine.—

* *The pretended impartial fpecimens of Mr. K's Review, as exhi-bited in the* Gentleman's Magazine.

T E M P E S T, Vol. I. p. 8.

Prof. to *Mir.*] Text. I have with fuch provifion in my art
So fafely ordered that there is no soul :
No not fo much perdition as an hair
Betid to any creature in the veffel.

tiality is left to the reader to determine, after having compared them with Mr. K's Review.

Rowe and *Warburton.*]　no foul *loſt*.
　　　　　Theobald.]　no *foil*.
　　　　　Johnſon.]　no *foil*.
　　　　　Kenrick.]　no *ill*.
Dr. Johnſon adopted *foil*, as co-inciding with what *Ariel* ſays afterwards :
　　　Not a hair periſhed
　　　On their ſuſtaining garments not a blemiſh.
　　Kenrick rejects *foil*, becauſe, as he ſays, it does not agree with *creature*, but relates to the cloaths only *.
　　　　　V O L. I. p. 9.
Proſ. to *Mir.*]　T E X T. —— and thy father
　　　Was duke of Milan, and his only heir,
　　　And princeſs, no worſe iſſued.
Theobald. A princeſs, no worſe iſſued.
Johnſon.　Perhaps it ſhould be, and *thou* his only heir.
Kenrick.　*Thou* deſtroys the meaſure ; *Theobald* is right †.
　　　　　V O L. I. p. 15.
Ariel.]　T E X T.　Reſtored by Johnſon.
　　　Not a ſoul
　　　But felt *a* fever of the *Mad*, and plaid
　　　Some tricks of deſpiration :
All modern editions, fever of the *mind*.
Kenrick.　*The* fever of the *mad* ‡.
　　　　　V O L. I. p. 19.
Mir.]　The ſtrangeneſs of your ſtory puts
　　　Heavineſs in me.
　　Mr. Kenrick cenſures Dr. Johnſon for attempting to account for a wonderful ſtory's producing ſleep, becauſe this heavineſs of *Miranda* was the effect of *Proſpero*'s enchantment, not conſidering that *Miranda*'s ſuppoſition was to be accounted for, not the fact §.

---

* This is a *falſe* repreſentation. Mr. K. does not require the text to be altered at all, and only propoſes this reading in caſe it ſhould be altered. He gives other and more ſubſtantial reaſons alſo in ſupport of his propoſal.
† *Falſe* again. The breach of the meaſure is not the only reaſon hinted by Mr. K. though that is a ſufficient one for rejecting Dr. Johnſon's *thou*.
‡ This too is *falſe*. Mr. K. approves the reading of all the later editions, viz. *a fever of the mind*, and only propoſes the changing of Dr. J's *a* into *the*, merely on the ſuppoſed neceſſity of altering the text, and the *poſſibility* of Shakeſpeare's writing *fever of the mad*.
§ Another lying blunder this ! It is not Miranda's childiſh notion that Mr. K. laughs at, but one of Dr. Johnſon's articles of faith ; who, in accounting for the ſaid notion, ſays, " I *believe* experience will prove that any violent agitation of the mind eaſily ſubſides in ſlumber."

As to the infinuations themfelves, they are indeed too invidious and contemptible to require any other an- fwer than may be deduced from the foregoing pages of this defence. But if Mr. Urban, and his brother criticks, will admit no man to have modefty or *virtue* but Dr. J. in whom even *indolence* and *infolence* is par- tially conceived to be fuch, they may know that Mr. K.

V O L. I. p. 38.

Ant.] TEXT. Although this Lord of weak remembrance
———— hath here almoft perfuaded,
For he's a fpirit of perfuafion, only
Profeffes to perfuade, the king, his fon's alive:
Johnfon. For HE, a fpirit of perfuafion, only
Profeffes to perfuade:
Kenrick retains the reading of the text, only removes the comma in the firft line from *perfuafion* to *only*; fuppofing the word *fpirit* to mean form, apparition, femblance, not the body, or fubftance of perfuafion.

V O L. I. p. 76.

Ariel. Text reftored by Dr. Warburton, and acquiefced in by Dr. Johnfon:
Where the bee fucks, there fuck I;
In a cowflip's bell I lie:
There I couch when owls do cry,
On the bat's back I do fly
After *fummer* merrily.
Theobald, Pope, and *Hanmer*, after *fun-fet.*
Kenrick endeavours to fhew, that the reafons given by Dr. Warburton for the reftoration are inconclufive †.
It is judged needlefs here to make any particular remarks on the above fpecimens, as their falfhood and partiality will be evident to every reader who compares the copy with the original.

† This indeed is true, and his endeavours are fufficiently fuccefsful. But can any thing be more flagrant than the above inftances of falfhood, pre- varication, and mifreprefentation? And yet it would be rude, indecent and unmannerly, I warrant ye, to charge Mr. Sylvanus Urban with telling *wilful lies* on this occafion. Yet are they any better? Modern politenefs, you will fay, requires me to fuit my ftile to the delicacy of the offender, rather than to the enormity of the crime. Well then, I tell you Dr. H——h " you are a fibber, fo you are, you, naughty man you, and I won't love you, nor will I give you any more marmalade or panada, fo I won't,"——Will this pleafe? or is it not fufficiently gentle and *candid?*

hath

hath at leaſt *pride* enough to be above *envying* any man, and *induſtry* enough to ſtand in no need of that *charity* which *idleneſs* muſt accept of or ſtarve †.

All the world knows the *Adventurer* languiſhed for a penſion, and long pined away at the diſappointment : nor will even his reputation ſupply its place, not-

† Not that the word *charity* is the moſt proper term to give to penſions beſtowed on thoſe who have repeatedly repreſented them as the wages of iniquity. But as I am willing to treat Dr. J. with all poſſible tenderneſs, I would not give it ſo ſevere a name, as is done by his pretended friends, who repreſent it as a ſort of huſh-money ; a kind of retaining fee, to prevent him engaging his pen in oppoſite intereſts. But, if this be the caſe, what is it better than a ſpecies of bribery and corruption ? And how does this differ from the wages of iniquity, except that ſuch wages are are received without being earned ? A mighty indelicate ſituation, after all, for a man of ſuch conſummate VIRTUE ! ——— But I cannot cloſe this note, without taking ſome notice of what is advanced on this ſubject, by the ſeveral *virtuous* critics who have cenſured Mr. K's performance.

They ſay Mr. K's great quarrel with Dr. J. appears to be the latter's accepting a penſion ; and yet they intimate the former would be glad of an opportunity of accepting one himſelf. But, pray, if theſe gentry know nothing of Mr. K as they pretend, how can they take upon them to ſay he would be ſo glad of a penſion ? And if they do know any thing of him, they muſt know at the ſame time, that, notwithſtanding Dr. J's *bon mot* *, his induſtry enables him to live much better, without a penſion, than Dr. J. can do with. Beſides, the caſe is not parallel ; for though a penſion might be acceptable to Mr. K. (and to whom, pray, would it not ?) he never railed at penſions, nor abuſed placemen and penſioners in his life ; and, if it were offered him, could receive it as a reward for ſervices done, or at leaſt intended to be done, to his country. But how a man of Dr. J's known political principles could receive it without a bluſh, and at the ſame time pretend to *modeſty* and *virtue*, is what I cannot conceive.

* To be added to the *Johnſoniana*, unleſs Mr. K. ſhould yield to the preſſing ſolicitations of Dr. J's friends, and be thence prevailed on to ſuppreſs thoſe *choice ſayings* in the next edition of his Review, as in all probability he will ; the authenticity of ſome of them being *ingenuouſly* queſtioned by the very people, from whoſe lips Mr. K. actually took them down.

withſtanding

withſtanding he may ſet an additional value on it *. But it is not for perſons of ſuch confined talents, and puſillanimous diſpoſitions, to judge of the motives and actions of writers of more extenſive knowledge and more manly abilities.

If any of Dr. J's partizans think they can defend him, in the late outrage he hath committed againſt the memory and reputation of Shakeſpeare, let them ſtand forth boldly, and they ſhall be received like men. But this, it ſeems, is not enough for the refined and elegant writers of the preſent age : they muſt be treated with *tenderneſs*, with *gentility*, with ſweatmeat and ſugar candy I warrant ye, like fine ladies and peeking children.——Out upon ſuch a pack of finicking fribbles ; with hearts in their bellies no bigger than pins heads, and thoſe even minnikins ; mere dealers in frippery in the rag-fair of Literature ! It is certainly a wonderful inſtance of a man's ſelf-ſufficiency to think himſelf able to encounter ſuch diminitive opponents as theſe ! Here, as Falſtaff ſays, is no vanity. Dean Swift uſed to ſay of himſelf, that he was too *proud* to be *vain*. I will venture, in this particular caſe, to ſay the ſame of the Reviewer of Dr Johnſon's Shakeſpeare : and ſo, Maſter Sylvanus, good night to your Urbanity ; and, to ſupper with what appetite you may.

---

* " And why ſhould he not ?" you will ſay. " Is not Dr. H, the editor of the immortal *Swift*, as Dr. J. is of *Shakeſpeare* ?"—— Yes, and hath doubtleſs done him equal honour in abſurdly and falſly criticiſing on the ſtile of that ſpirited and admirable writer. Oh ! if the ghôſt of *Swift* did but haunt Dr. H. as that of Shakeſpeare does Dr. J. How would that ſarcaſtic ſpirit avenge himſelf on this piddling critick !

S E C T.

S E C T. VII.

Remarks on the strictures of the Candid Reviewers, and the other volunteer criticks that have taken upon them to abuse the Reviewer of Dr. J's Shakespeare.

IT is something remarkable that, among all the writers, who have drawn the pen on the present occasion, against Mr. K. not one of them hath ventured to take the part of Dr. J. The *critical* Reviewers, we have seen, give him up entirely ; even Mr. Urban himself says nothing in his defence. The pretended acrimony of Mr. K's manner, indeed, is disapproved by all parties ; but this I have already endeavoured to justify. I shall proceed, therefore, to enquire how far those, which are as yet unnoticed, are justifiable in *their* manner of treating Mr. K.—To begin with the *Candid* Reviewers. These *honest* gentlemen, who have borrowed the whole of Mr. K's preface, as they did the month before the greater part of Dr. J's, have given such an inconsistent and motley account of the *Reviewer's* performance, that it is very difficult to say whether they have most praised or censured it.

In its *favour* they sometimes admit, that " the matter of it does demand the highest approbation." That " Dr. Johnson will find himself *unable* to reply to it."—That " Mr. Kenrick has very sufficiently shewn that Dr. Johnson has played booty throughout his boasted edition."—That " Mr. K. hath improved upon Dr. J."—That " they agree with Mr. K. that

Shakespeare

Shakefpeare ftill ftands as much in need of a new edition as ever."—That " he hath happily fucceeded in
giving, by means of an eafy interpretation, a confiftent meaning to feveral paffages, in regard to which
other interpreters have run after far-fetched explica-
tions."—That " they entirely agree with him in the
fimple fenfe he gives to words, and join with him in
wondering how Warburton and others could ever puz-
zle themfelves fo much about them," &c. &c.

In its *disfavour*, they infinuate that " Mr. K. has
committed blunders as well as other men, who bragged
as much, witnefs poor Dr. Warburton."—That " Mr.
K. has fometimes mifapprehended his author's meaning,
as well as Dr. Johnfon."—That " future obfervers
will improve on Mr. K, and that he is therefore not
fit to publifh an edition of Shakefpeare."—That " Mr.
K. inftead of profiting by his own admonitions, fometimes commits the fame faults he blames in others."—
That they cannot help expreffing " their admiration
at the bleffed effects which metaphyfics and philofophy
have upon criticifm in poetry!" intimating thereby
that Mr. K. is too much of a philofopher to know any
thing of poetry.—That Mr. K. difplays great inability
in tracing out the beauty of poetic images, and that
his remarks are ridiculous.

I fhall not enter upon a confutation of the affertions
of thefe critics; the inftances in which they prefume
to differ from Mr. K. being, to the laft degree, ab-
furd and contemptible; as the reader may conclude
from their affirming, in the courfe of their critical inveftigation, that Shakefpeare had no knowledge of a

G   *climax,*

climax, which they are pleafed to term a rhetorical gorgon-faced word. They have fagacioufly difcovered alfo that Shakefpeare acted, with *very little* judgment, in the execution of one of his greateft mafter-pieces of art. But this is fufficient with regard to their literary ftrictures : I come now to their perfonal ones ; and here they charge Mr. K. with having defcended to make ufe of " fcurrility, abufive and even low-lived * petulance," with " ribaldry," with " bragging," with " foul language," with " being habituated to abufive bluftering," with " wanting a penfion to ftop his mouth," with " being a voracious boreas," with " being a literary bruifer," with " fighting tooth and nail

* Does not this polite epithet ferve to fhew, that the writer himfelf muft undoubtedly be a perfon in *high-life ? Ex ungue leonem.* This critic, to fpeak in his own dialect, muft certainly be a gentleman of *three outs.* Low-lived ! Could ever one have thought of fuch a word's getting into print, and that by means of a profeffed critic too ! *O tempora ! O mores !* Proud, however, as this gentleman may be of the *Dignity and Advantages of living in a Garret* *, I would not advife him to riot too luxurioufly on rich fauces. Spartan broth is a ftimulating aliment, efpecially when feafoned with garlick. Thofe who live *high* feldom live *long.* Nay, my mind forebodes that, even while I am now writing, this fon of *Candour* is no more. The death-watch ticks — 'tis even fo — hark, I hear his knell — poor devil ! His fpirit is departed. 'Twere a dirty piece of work, or I would rip him up, and preferve his carcafe, like that of Duke Humphry, in pickle. If any charitable hand will do it for him, it muft be fteeped well in the acrimony of Mr. K's Review. That may poffibly keep it awhile above-ground. But alas ! what pickle can long preferve a body, that, for want of proper ftamina, never was wholly alive ; and, by the time it was half dead, was quite rotten ! Afhes to afhes ; dirt unto dirt ; fuch is the end of modern *candour !*

* See an ingenious pamphlet, publifhed fome years ago, with this title.

like

like dogs and bears," and finally with " being a whim-
fical, lynx-eyed, critico-poetico-metaphyfico-magico
philofopher."

The reader will judge for himfelf how far a fet of
critics, who are fo admirably well fkilled in calling
names, are to be credited in charging any writer with
fcurrility, petulance, ribaldry, and *foul-language*; words,
I can affure him, that are not to be found in Mr. K's
Review! But it is not only againft fuch critics, as
pretend to have read his performance, that Mr. K.
hath juft caufe of complaint. There are thofe who
condemn both him and his Review, without feeing or
knowing any thing of either, except what is told them
by Dr. Johnfon's partizans. Nay, feveral of thefe
candid and *impartial* gentry began to rail openly in the
public news-papers, at fight of Mr. K's advertifement
only. The terms of this, truly, were highly indecent; it was a kind of high-treafon, a fpecies of impiety, even to imagine Dr. Johnfon could be *ignorant*
or *inattentive.* One would have thought him placed
at the head of literature, as the Roman pontiff is at
the head of his church, and with the fame pretenfions
to infallibility. Every body, forfooth, was expected
to kifs pope Johnfon's toe, even at the hazard of having their fore-teeth kicked out by his holinefs's bruta-
lity. But Mr. K. had never any inclination to be treated
in fo grofs a manner, as that in which he had heard
Dr. J. had taken the liberty to behave towards fome perfons of the firft rank in the world of fcience and letters.
It was referved for him, indeed, to pay the doctor in
his own coin, and avenge the repeated infults received

by

by injured modefty. To appeal to fact, however, in fupport of what is above afferted, Mr. K's Review was hardly publifhed before a letter, figned *J. May,* appeared in the London Chronicle, evidently founded on the advertifement only, in which Mr. K. was charged in grofs terms with making ufe of FOUL-MOUTHED *language,* of want of *decency, good-manners,* and I know not what.—What a *fine-mouthed,* fmooth-tongued, polifhed generation is the prefent! This Mr. Sweet-lips was pleafed to fay, " Whatever judgment the public may entertain of the late edition of Shakefpeare, the editor is too well known, to have the charge of ignorance fo eafily admitted againft him."—Doubtlefs he is ; and it would in no fhape have anfwered the Reviewer's end for the public to have been fatisfied by his advertifement without reading his book.—By the readinefs, however, with which Mr. May, and indeed all Dr. J's friends, feem to give up the editor of Shakefpeare, there is great reafon to prefume Mr. K. did not promife more in the news-papers than he effected in his pamphlet. So that it appears Dr. J. is not fo well *known* as this gentleman fuppofes. His name, indeed, is in every body's mouth, and it is poffible there are few of thofe, whom, from their fondnefs for *fine writers,* we may with propriety enough call *fine readers,* who have not yawned with drowfy admiration over thofe quaint and infipid performances, *Irene* and the *Idler.* But thefe works fupport but a fmall part of Dr. Johnfon's literary reputation : the foundation of which is laid fo deep in the rubbifh of erudition, that it is impoffible

poffible for fuch fuperficial readers to difcover it.
Like the fpectator of the invifible cock, however,
Mr. *May* feems to be very fure it is there.—This
fame Mr. J. May, alfo, takes farther upon him to afk
" who is this W. K. who fo rudely fteps forth from
" — nobody knows where, to attack a gentleman of
" known literary abilities ?"—This gentleman muft
have very few connections, and know little of what is
doing, in the literary world, to have any occafion to
afk fuch a queftion. For, whoever *he* be, or where-
ever *he* comes from, Mr. K. may certainly fay with
propriety to HIM, *Not to know me argues thyfelf un-
known.* But perhaps this gentleman, like the editor
of Lloyd's Chronicle, and fome other writers, who affected, on the like occafion, to fpeak of *one Mr. K.*
as if an utter ftranger to his exiftence, may only know
him too well, having before fmarted from the juft feverity of his critical pen. If fo, Mr. May is anfwered ;
if not, and he was really defirous of knowing fomething of Mr. K. he may have, in fome meafure, gra-
tified his curiofity in the perufal of the foregoing
fheets.

The next gentleman I fhall take notice of (which
fhall be the laft, as there would be no end of purfuing
anonymous writers) is one Mr. Hypercriticus, who,
about the fame time, without ever having feen Mr. K's
book, was incited to publifh, among other fagacious
reflections, the following wife fentences. " From the
" very fhort time fince the publication of Mr. John-
" fon's edition of Shakefpeare, and from the very ra-
" pid

" pid * progreſs of Mr. Kenrick's remarks thereon, I
" *believe* they muſt be crude and imperfect." Believe!
quoth he, Is not this very candid and ingenuous?
But he proceeds to give a reaſon for the faith that is
in him. " For to paſs a right judgment on books
" (ſays Longinus) requires a great length of time, and
" a perfect knowledge of the ſubject." Well, and
what then? The writings of Shakeſpeare might have
been the object of Mr. K's ſtudy for years, and he
might thence have acquired (at leaſt for what Hypercriticus knew to the contrary) a perfect knowledge of
the ſubject; and if ſo, no longer time would be re-
quiſite for him to point out Dr. Johnſon's miſtakes,
than was neceſſary to read his book. But, ſays this
gentleman, " I *ſuppoſe* Mr. K. is a critick by intui-
" tion ; one who, in regard to books, ſees into the
" merit of the whole, by reading only a part." As
we had before a *believe*, here we have a *ſuppoſe*. Are
not theſe very pretty grounds to proceed on, to the
condemnation of a writer unread. But how, if what
I juſt now aſſerted be true, that Shakeſpeare's writings
have been many years the favourite object of Mr.
K's reading and ſtudy ; how, if he hath long ſince
accumulated materials for an edition of that poet, as

---

* Another of Dr. J's friends is angry with Mr. K. for a like
reaſon, remarking, as before obſerved, that Mr. K. *ſtans pede in
uno* wrote his Review of Dr. Johnſon's book, before a perſon of
a moderate capacity could read it.—But if Mr. K. is generally in
the right, and Dr. J. in the wrong, I don't ſee how this reflects
any diſgrace on the former. On the contrary, if Mr. K. *ſtans
pede in uno* hath given ſuch a broad footed coloſſus as Dr. J. a fall,
it ſhews him to be no bad wreſtler. So ſtand clear, if you are
upon the *offenſive*.—

is

is also true; I say, how, Mr. Hypercriticus, in this case, can you justify your precipitate censures, and what becomes of your *suppose?* And to suppose for once it was not so, surely Mr. K. might, as you say, judge of the *whole* by reading a *part*, with as much propriety as you judge of his performance by reading only his advertisement in the news-papers? Why might not he be, without a *suppose*, a critick intuitively as well as you? But " sarcasm, you say, is unmannerly." I wish, that where you learned to be so very *mannerly*, you had only learned also to be equally *ingenuous*; you would have saved me the trouble, and yourself the mortification, of this reprehension. I say the same to all the rest of the mannerly, candid, decent, delicate partizans of Dr. Johnson, who have, on this occasion, been attempting to box in mufflers, or throwing dirt with their gloves on. As to the former, Mr. K. is too hardy to feel their puny efforts to offend him; and, as to the latter he cannot help smiling to see, how easily their pellets dry and rub out, while they themselves are begrimed up to the ears, in vainly endeavouring to befpatter him.

Having now done with particular altercation, I should here leave both Mr. K. and Dr. J. to stand or fall by the judgment of the publick, had there not been some strictures let fall in some of the papers levelled against Mr. K. charging him with as great a want of *modesty*, as he hath done Dr. J. with want of *knowledge*. I shall therefore beg leave to say a word or two on both these topicks, viz. on the *modesty of men of letters*, and on *literary knowledge*.

S E C T.

SECT. VIII.

On the modesty of men of letters.

OF all kinds of *modesty*, whether real or affected, perhaps that of *Authors* is the moft fingular. *A modest Author!* It is a kind of contradiction in terms, and founds to my ear exactly like the expreffion of a *modest strumpet.* There is no doubt that a man may be a modeft man before he commence writer, as a gentleman may be an honeft gentleman before he be made minifter-of-ftate, or as even a butcher may have fome bowels of compaffion before he turn bum bailiff; but no fooner are they initiated into the *routine* of their refpective offices, than modefty, honefty, and humanity take flight and leave them.

This is fevere, you will fay.—It is fo; but it is neverthelefs founded in truth, and may be applied to many writers now living, and probably likely to live fo long as they can get any thing by proftituting either their talents or reputation.

Certain it is, that a clofer parallel can hardly be drawn between any two known characters, than between a common fcribbler and a common ftrumpet. How bafhfully doth the young enamorato of the mufes look at you, when you fpeak to him about publifhing his firft production; even as an innocent countrywench blufhes up to the eyes, when you firft talk of untying her garter! But when they have been a while tumbled over in the fheets, the virgin-modefty
of

of both is pretty equal. There is this difference between them, indeed, that the one grows bold by lo-
fing reputation, and the other by gaining it. This
difference, however, does not in the leaft alter their
conduct or appearance when they come upon the town:
the reputation then aimed at by both, being very different from what they either loft or gained. The one
feeks not to improve his talents any more than the
other her charms ; but both apply affiduoufly to difplay and make the moft of what they poffefs ; and
if they covet fame, it is generally with a fecondary
view to the venal purpofes of proftitution *. Is it poffible that fuch characters can have any real modefty,
however neceffary they may find it to affume its appearance, artfully to impofe on the world ?

Not but that there are degrees, both in venality
and impudence ; fo that as a *demi-rep* may be *compara-
tively* modeft and difinterefted, fo may an *author*. But
to drop the comparifon ; as there are many writers of
a more liberal ftamp than to come under any deno-
mination that will rank them in this parallel ; writers,
who, while they labour to inftruct and entertain the
publick, labour equally to improve themfelves, and to
render their future writings more valuable from the en-

* Thus an author, whofe abilities are exhaufted, and a cour-
tezan, whofe charms are decayed, may ftill live upon the emolu-
ments arifing from their fame. Let them but get their names
recorded in a *Race* ‡, or a *Meretriciad*, and they may ftill remain
the favourites of purblind fops and fuperficial witlings.

‡ See a poem fo called, in which Dr. J. is celebrated, among other
things, for his *modefty* ; and in like manner Paul V——t, who wears a little
fmart bob, is defcribed as overwhelmed by a wig more tremendous than Dal-
mahoy's.

courage-

couragement given to the prefent, I muft own I cannot help thinking that fuch writers debafe themfelves greatly, whenever they affect the falfe modefty of unexperienced tyros, or defigning ignorants. There is a fpecies of affurance in men of real knowledge, which may be faid, without impropriety, to be confiftent with the modefty becoming their character, as they could not poffibly diveft themfelves of it without evident hypocrify and affectation. As to authors by profeffion, they muft neceffarily either difplay their affurance by infifting on their own merit, or, in fact, confefs themfelves bunglers, or impoftors. And indeed why fhould they not? If an artift difcover any mode of mechanical operation, or execute a piece of mechanifm, which is an improvement on what others have done before him, or what nobody can execute but himfelf, who charges him with want of modefty in boldly afferting his own pre-eminence? Why then fhould a critick, a philofopher, an hiftorian, or a poet, be thought too affuming in laying publick claim to that merit, which they actually poffefs? What fhould we think of an artizan or manufacturer, who fhould, in his advertifements and fhop-bills, *modeftly* affect a diffidence of being able to give his cuftomers fatisfaction, having himfelf a mean opinion of his own abilities? Should we not conclude, without hefitation, that he was either a knave or fool, or both? Yet how common is it to meet with authors, who have been many years *in trade*, ridiculoufly affecting to think meanly of productions, which they neverthelefs importunately obtrude on the publick, and make us pay for at as high

a

a price as poſſible? Yet many of theſe writers have the character of being modeſt men. In my opinion, however, I think it an inſtance of very great *impudence*, to ſay no worſe of it, for a man to offer me a commodity at a great price, and to tell me at the ſame time he thinks it good for little. For what is this, in fact, but to tell me that he thinks me as great a fool as he confeſſes himſelf to be a knave?

And yet, if a writer were to uſe the ſame arguments in the preface of his book, to ſet off his works to advantage, as an artizan or manufacturer is allowed to do his, in his ſhop or warehouſe, he would of courſe be condemned for want of *modeſty*. Thus we ſee a very modeſt man may incur the obloquy of being an impudent author; and a very impudent author acquire the reputation of being a modeſt man.

The true ſtate of this matter ſeems to be this. Ignorance and impudence as generally go together as innocence and modeſty; but ignorance being often the companion, and ſometimes even the guardian, of innocence, it is no wonder that impudence ſhould put on the appearance of modeſty, in order to make us take mere ignorance for pure innocence.

Knowledge as naturally inſpires fortitude, as truth abominates hypocriſy. How abſurd is it then to require men of real abilities to affect that diffidence and ignorance to which they muſt neceſſarily be ſtrangers! At the ſame time, what can we think of thoſe writers, who, after being long hackneyed in the ways of men, and of their profeſſion; who, after ſetting themſelves up even at the head of that profeſſion, pretend

H 2 *to*

to tremble while they write, to bow down with reverential awe to superior learning, to kiss the rod of correction, &c. &c. What, I say, can we think of such writers, but that, sensible of their own ignorance or imbecillity, they are cajoling the publick in a manner that deserves the name of the highest *impudence*.

Much more modest and manly is it for a writer of years and experience, to assert boldly and confidently what he hath good reason to think he knows *; and openly to defy every groundless imputation or insinuation of ignorance.

S E C T. IX.

On literary knowledge; with some remarks on IGNORANCE *and* INATTENTION.

IT hath been frequently observed, that the knowledge of *words* is not the knowledge of *things*. Indeed the distinction between the *scholar* and the man of *science* is now become general. It is nevertheless certain, that a man cannot be a considerable proficient in philology, particularly with regard to the modern languages, without having made some acquisitions in science. It is not my intent, however, to expatiate here on this distinction, or to enhance the preference due to science above mere literature; my intention be-

* And if he has not such reason, he should not trouble the publick with his reveries.

ing

ing only to throw out a few fhort obfervations on literary knowledge in general.

" Be not vain of thy learning, child, faid my grand-
" father to me when I was a boy; I have lived to for-
" get more than thou haft learned in thy whole life."
All this was very true; and yet I thought myfelf, neverthelefs, as good a fcholar as my grandfather: for
when we were fometimes both at a lofs for a word or
two of Greek, I found the only difference between us
was, that I turned to the Lexicon for thofe I never
knew, and he for thofe he could not remember: but
my *copia verborum* was neverthelefs equal to his.

Now it would be a matter of fome importance to
determine, whether a man can with propriety be faid
to know what he cannot remember, even though he
fhould have formerly had it perfectly impreffed in his
memory?

I am afraid that we fhall go nigh to be laughed at
by the vulgar, fhould we admit that a man may be
faid to know what he hath forgot, and can't tell us if
we ask him. And yet, if he fhould recollect it half-
an-hour hence, without any body's telling him in the
mean time, furely he muft have had fuch knowledge
in him at the time of his being asked; fince it does
not appear that he had by any external means acquired
it fince.

This would afford a curious and fubtle difqufition;
but, as I have not time to enter here into a profound
inveftigation of all the difficulties that fuggeft themfelves
concerning it, I fhall only make an application of it to the
learning

learning of the two laſt editors of Shakeſpeare, and leave the reader to make it out as well as he can.

Mr. K. hath proved, in ſeveral parts of his Review of Dr. J's edition, that the ſaid editor either did not then know, or had forgot the meaning of ſeveral words and paſſages, which it is plain the Doctor muſt have formerly known, and probably would have recollected ſome odd time or other. I ſhall inſtance only one or two. In one the very learned Doctors J. and W. both appear not to know the meaning of the word *convene* ; Dr. W. objecting to Shakeſpeare's proper uſe of it, and Dr. J. adopting the ſaid objection : and yet Mr. K. hath juſtified Shakeſpeare, and convicted both the editors on the authority of Dr. J's own Dictionary.

Again, in regard to the uſe of the old phraſe, *taken with the manner*, both theſe learned editors flatly contradict themſelves ; aſſerting in one volume that it is uſed one way, and in another volume that it is uſed differently.

I might mention many other inſtances of the like kind ; but theſe will ſuffice for my preſent purpoſe. What I want to know is, whether theſe are inſtances of *ignorance* or not ?

Dr. J's friends will ſay, " O, no — he certainly knew better." Knew better ? when ? What, when he was told of the blunder, I ſuppoſe ? Surely that man may juſtly be called *ignorant*, whoſe knowledge, how great ſoever, is out of the way when it is wanted !

Will it be ſaid, theſe are not inſtances of *ignorance* but *inattention* ? Pray what is *inattention* ? Do you

mean

mean to fay that the Doctor did not read thefe paffages, or that he read them when he was afleep?

If he read them, and was wide awake, thefe miftakes could never have happened from *inattention*, but
muft have been derived from *forgetfulnefs*; which,
according to the arguments above adduced, muft be a
fpecies at leaft of *ignorance*.

But the criticks will poffibly afk me, what I mean
by being *wide awake*, and by Dr. J's *reading* thefe
paffages? They will fay, perhaps, that they know as
well as I, that, when a commentator reads a paffage
over, he muft comprehend it fome way or other, right
or wrong; and that no *inattention*, in that cafe, can
prevent the operation of his judgment refpecting the
words that lie before him; fo that, if he then miftakes, it muft be through *ignorance*. "But this was
"not the cafe; (it may be faid) Dr. J. could never
"dream that Dr. W. could be miftaken fo grofly in
"matters fo clear and obvious, and therefore copied
"thofe paffages implicitly from Dr. W's Comment:
"fo that it was nothing more than *inattention*."

Call you this method of proceeding *inattention*? It
is fuch *wilful negligence*, that your friend Dr. J. will
hardly be obliged to you for thus defending him from
the charge of *ignorance*; for furely, if we may not
call it want of *knowledge*, we muft call it want of ——
fomething elfe, which a man of acknowledged *virtue*
fhould not be without. What would a fimilar conduct to this, be called in any of the common con-
cerns of life? Happy is it, undoubtedly, for the prefent race of authors, that they ALL, *being penfioned*,

can

can fubfift and provide for their families, without being obliged to publifh their works by fubfcription ; for,
after fuch flagrant inftances of *inattention*, and that in
a writer of the firft reputation for learning and *virtue*,
what encouragement can any other, of lefs note, or
lefs reputed virtue, ever hope to meet with ?

The late Mr. Fielding, fpeaking fomewhere of thofe
gentlemen, who had tied themfelves up, as it was then
called, from fubfcribing to works of genius and literature, expreffes his refentment againft them, by fay-
ing, it is a pity they were not tied up in good earneft ;
but what do thofe authors deferve, who firft gave occafion for people entering into fuch illiberal engage-
ments ?

And what doth Dr. J. in particular deferve, for
having obtruded on the world the worft Commentary
of Shakefpeare that ever appeared ? and, at the fame
time, for having, by his procraftination and neglect,
fo effectually difgufted the publick with editors and
fubfcriptions, that it is prefumed the ableft commentator in the kingdom would find little encouragement
for a fimilar undertaking ? notwithftanding, as the
criticks juftly obferve, SHAKESPEARE *ftands* NOW *in*
more need of a NEW EDITION *than ever*.

R. R.

POST-

POSTSCRIPT,

MONTHLY REVIEWERS.

I Cannot help thinking it a little fortunate, gentlemen, that your obfervations on Mr. K's Review appeared before the printer had quite finifhed the foregoing fheets ; as it affords me an opportunity of adding a word or two, by way of reply, to your obfervations on his *extraordinary* Review. It is indeed not without reafon you give it that appellation ; but, pray, do you mean thereby to infinuate that nobody hath a right to make ufe of the word *Review* but yourfelves ? Have you an exclufive privilege to it, like that which is laid to the *Poft*, or to the *Gazette ?*

It is true, that you *monthly* gentlemen have the right of prior occupancy over your periodical rivals ; who deal, like yourfelves, in the wholefale branch of criticifm. But, becaufe you are wholefale dealers, are you therefore to be monopolizers ? Muft every Review extraordinary be ftigmatized as an extraordinary Review, becaufe it is not fabricated or vended in your work-fhop or warehoufe ?

It was, doubtlefs, horridly provoking, to have your work taken out of your hands, and difpatched, while

I you

you were whetting your edge-tools. But why, therefore, find fault with the tools of another artizan,
whofe work you do not feem to difapprove fo much,
as his manner of executing it ? Surely Dr. J. might as
well fuffer by a Tomahawk as a cleaver! Is it not as
well to be fcalped by a Mohawk, as to be knocked
on the head, or have one's throat cut, by a carcafe-
butcher ? And pray, how do you differ from the
fanguinary affaffins of White-chapel and Cow-crofs,
except that yours are intellectual, and theirs are animal victims ? They only mangle the body. You
mortify the very foul ; and muft expect to be morti-
fied in turn. For let me tell you, in the firft place,
that even your witty conceit of comparing Mr. K. to
a Mohawk or a Cherokee, will never be thought your
own, by thofe who recollect the Cherokees and Iro-
quois that Bifhop W. is charged with having fet on
the back of Dr. Lowth. You critical gentlemen feem
indeed to be all terribly miftaken with regard to the
place of Mr. K's nativity. The *Critical* Reviewers
and Chroniclers declared him to be a *Tartar*, and you
infift upon his being a Mohawk or a Cherokee Indian.
It is a pretty long poft-ftage from the defarts of Tar-
tary to the wilds of America. We know, indeed, that
you fpeak metaphorically, and, tho' far-fetched, fo far it
is excufable; but let us fee if the hyperbole is not to be
found among your other tropes and figures. You fay
" the *Reviewer* (Mr. K.) feems to be one of thofe vi-
" olent affailants, whofe aim is not merely to vanquifh,
" but even to *exterminate* his antagonift." It is well
you put in that qualifying *feems.* But you fay pofitively,
that

that he endeavours to expofe his antagonift as a very *pretender* to all literature and fcience.

This, you fay, is quite outrageous.—And fo it might be, were it ftrictly true ; but you will pleafe to obferve, Mr. K. does not *pofitively deny* that Dr. Johnfon is mafter of the languages and fciences ; he only fays, it *does not appear* fo to *him*. Who knows but Mr. K. might here modeftly intend to infinuate his own inability to comprehend the amazing ftores and vaft profundity of Dr. Johnfon's fcience and erudition ? Why then would you not give him credit for the appearance of being in fo mild and promifing a difpofition * ? Be this, however, as it may, you are certainly miftaken in fuppofing that Mr. K. hath queftioned the abilities of Dr. J. as a man of fcience, a critick and philologift, merely becaufe the Doctor, as you fay, miftook his talents in undertaking an edition of Shakefpeare. In reading the preceding fheets,

---

* And that thefe criticks might juftly have done it, had they been inclined to fhew Mr. K. fair play, will appear fufficiently from the paffage hinted at, with the note he hath annexed. " I do not fay," fays Mr. K. " that Dr. Johnfon may not pro- " bably be well fkilled in *fome* things ; not that *I know* that he is " well fkilled in any * ; for, though I have read *all* his *works*, I " declare he does not *appear to me* (at leaft fo far as I myfelf am " able to judge) to be *mafter* of any *one fcience*, or any *one lan-* " *guage*. Not that I *deny* him to be mafter of the *whole circle of* " *fciences*, and of *all languages ancient and modern*."—Surely, Mr. Monthly Reviewer, it is you that are *outrageous!* for Mr. K. fpeaks here with becoming modefty and diffidence.

---

* I will except, indeed, the article of *literary compofition* ; in which, fo far as the merit of a fpeech, an effay, a life, or a novel, goes, he is undoubtedly the beft writer in Chriftendom.

you

you will have feen that, although the violation of
Shakefpeare was the firft fault for which the Doctor
happens to be publickly arraigned, it was by no means
the firft fact in which he had been caught, and for
which he would, fooner or later, have certainly been
indicted, by his prefent profecutor.

But I fee how the matter ftands with you, periodical
criticks. Your own credit refts on too tottering a
bafis for you to indulge yourfelves fafely in any inclination you might have to chaftife writers of *eftablifhed
reputation*. You are therefore reduced, in a manner,
to the neceffity of difplaying your dexterity in the
manual exercife of the critical fcourge, on objects
juft ftriving to go alone, without any body to
fupport them. This behaviour, doubtlefs, redounds
greatly to the honour of your prowefs and mag-
nanimity; and as the notice I here take of it, may
poffibly have fome little effect on your cenforial
dignity, if not on the intereft of your proprietor, I
fhall take the liberty of giving both him and you a
word of advice, for the regulation of your future conduct. I muft own indeed that the Monthly Review,
from its regularity in coming to town for fo many
years, full or empty, hath obtained the reputation of
being one of the moft refpectable ftage-coaches on the
high-road of Parnaffus; but Mr. G——h, (that is,
Mr. *Gee ho*, the driver) will give me leave to tell him,
that, if he continues to detain his paffengers fuch a
confounded while at Turnham-green, clogging his
wheels fo curfedly with the coom of dullnefs, to make
them run fmooth, fome other *Jehu*, on the fame road,

will

will infallibly fet up a poft-coach with fteel fprings, that will beat him hollow. It is, befides, almoft become fcandalous now to have the beft place in this carriage; for, look at their horfes; no fewer than fix of them, you fee; but how they're matched! black, white, and pye-bald! lame, blind, and fpavin'd! The very picture of the mock-cavalcade of the Grand Mafons! Then you fee the two fore-horfes drag the whole team! An Hammerfmith ftage, tugged by a horfe and a half, gets a mile a head of them before they reach Hyde-park-corner. I, myfelf, have even fometimes rode on the coach-box, when Gee-ho, being a good-natured fellow, would let me hold the reins for half-an-hour or fo: but I might cry *auy*, *auy*, till my lungs burft, before I could mend their pace. It was, indeed, a miracle to me, that we ever got in time to town, when I obferved that no two horfes ever pulled together, and more than one of them hung an arfe, and drawed backwards all the way.

But to drop the allegory.

You fpeak of Mr. K's having treated Dr. J. with extraordinary *freedoms*.—Pray, Sir, who is Dr. J. that Mr. K. may not treat him, at his own peril, with as much freedom as he pleafes? If S. J. be *artium magifter*, W. K. is *philofophiæ doctor*, and fo far upon a footing. If S. J. be L. L. D., W. K. is J. U. D. If Mr. K. alfo was not educated at the univerfities that complimented him with his degrees, Dr. J. ftands in the fame predicament with regard to thofe learned feminaries that dignified him with his. There is, to be fure, this difference between the two doctors, that the

latter

latter never has thought it worth while, like the former, to advertife fuch infignificant circumftances in
the magazines and news-papers, holding in very flight
eftimation fuch literary endowments, as may be pur-
chafed at a Scotch univerfity for ten pounds; at almoft any German one for twenty ducats; and may be
had, as Dr. H. knows, from L——th, merely at the
moving folicitation of a printer.

Again, you ask, Sir, whether Mr. K. is not apprehenfive, on account of his feverity, of fharing the fate
of Tom Ofborne? That is, in plain terms, of Dr. J's
knocking him down. This is, to be fure, a very concife
and *liberal* method of determining literary merit, and
poffibly may have fome effect on the Monthly Reviewers. This intimidating intimation, indeed, may
in fome meafure ferve to account for the tremendous
influence of Dr J's perfonal and literary authority in general. For who will hefitate to commend, or dare to
contend againft, a writer poffeffed of fuch *knock-me-
down* * arguments? You will pleafe to take this along
with you, however, that, although Mr. K. may not
have fuch terrific talents, nor be quite fo much of a
brute † as many more celebrated writers, he may pof-

* See Foote's Minor.

† See an ingenious copy of verfes, lately publifhed in the St.
James's Chronicle, wherein the Dr. is proved, on the confeffion of
his own friends, to be, indeed, the *Prince of beafts*; a conclufion at
which neither Dr. J. nor his friends could reafonably take offence, one of them having thought proper, in a copy of verfes
before printed in the fame paper, very politely to compare Mr.
K. and his friends to a parcel of *monkies*; and, at the fame time,
to liken the furly grumbling of the Dr. himfelf to the contemptuous
growling of the *lion*. This verfifier, however, affords not the *firft*
example, wherein the ear of pufillanimity hath been deceived by
the

I

fibly be found, on trial, as much of a *man*, in every
refpect, as the beft of them.

Could you imagine then, Mr. *Monthly*, that Mr. K.
would not refent that partiality which you have evidently betrayed in your remarks on *his* Review. This
partiality is the more evident from your very different and favourable conftruction of the ftile and manner of a pamphlet recently publifhed againft one of
the gentlemen attacked by Mr. K. I mean Dr. L—th's
Letter to Dr. W————n ; the acrimony, feverity,
and fcurrility of which are, in every refpect, much
greater than is to be found in the ftrictures of Mr. K.
on Dr. J. And yet this is with you the *elegant* and
unexceptionable production of a *gentle* and amiable writer, difplaying equally the abilities of the fcholar and
the gentleman. Nay, you yourfelf, Mr. Critick,
have quoted fome paffages, wherein the language and
allufions are as *low* as poffible, and, indeed, hardly
grammatical. What do you think of this writer's ac-
cufing a bifhop of the church, in plain terms, with
having been guilty " of *fneering* at the original Scrip-
" tures ; with making ufe of far-fetched conceit and
" forced pleafantry, void of wit, of meaning, of
" common fenfe, and *common decency* : with ufing
" low banter, illiberal burlefque upon the prophets,
" the apoftles, and the holy Scriptures." You will

the braying of an afs in a lion's fkin. How far Dr. J. may be
compared to fuch an animal fo difguifed, time will fhew, Mr. K.
not having begun to ftrip off that fkin, but with a determined
refolution to exhibit the real creature, fooner or later, in *puris
naturalibus.*

pleafe

pleaſe to obſerve, that ſuch a charge as this, brought
againſt ſuch a character, is not only ſcurrilous, but,
if falſe, is, to the laſt degree, baſe and injurious. And,
pray, how is the truth of ſuch problematic accuſations
to be proved ? Who is to judge whether the paſſages,
hinted at in Dr. W's writings be ſuch *low banter* and
illiberal burleſque or not ? Is Dr. L— himſelf to judge
of this, or you, Mr. Monthly Reviewer ? Give me
leave to ſay, you will find no ſuch *equivocal* accuſations brought by Mr. K. againſt Dr. J. If he hath
charged him with being *ignorant* and *inattentive*, he
hath given repeated proofs of the truth of his aſſer-
tion. If he hath called Dr. J. *indolent, ſelf-ſufficient,*
or *arrogant*, is he not notoriouſly all theſe ? If Mr. K.
hath, at any time, ſuggeſted the Doctor's want of *ap-*
prehenſion or *invention*, he hath in like manner proved
it. After all which, I would be glad to know where
is the illiberality or ſcurrility of Mr. K's laughing at
him, and calling him *dull* ; nay, even though he
ſhould inſinuate that he hath no more imagination than
a leaden plummet, and ſay he was the *dulleſt animal of*
all commentators. For, pray, where is the harm of all
this, even whether it be true or falſe ? That the Doctor
is a commentator, ſuch a one as he is, nobody will
deny : that he is an *animal*, and a very ſtrange one
too, every body will own : and, as *dullneſs*, even in the
higheſt or loweſt degree, is by no means criminal, I cannot ſee how reflections of this kind can be, with any con-
ſiſtent pretence to impartiality, be deemed illiberal and
ſcurrilous by criticks, who have admitted the above
inſtance, quoted from Dr. L. to be elegant, refined,

or

or polite. It is true that Mr. K. hath ftrongly infi-
nuated, that Dr. J. hath not done juftice either to his
fubfcribers, or to the proprietors, in his edition of
Shakefpeare : And hath not he proved it? Nay, doth
not the event of its publication fufficiently fhew that
he had no need to have given himfelf the trouble to
prove what all the world admit to be true? If, on
this account, he hath treated Dr. J. feverely, the Doctor
hath juft the fame right of complaint as a pickpocket,
who gets only horfe whipped, or pumped, inftead of
a feverer punifhment. Ought not the Doctor to do as
he does, fhake his ears, flink quietly off, and think
himfelf happy *it is no worfe?*

It is true Mr. K. hath charged Dr. J. with an invidious defign of detracting from the moral and religious
character of Shakefpeare. But in what manner has he
done this?—Not by a mere verbally-abufive declara-
tion of the fact in general ; but by a fpirited and fair
allegation, fupported by particular teftimonies.

And yet, notwithftanding all this, Mr. K. truly, is with
you an *Orlando Furiofo* in criticifm, a very *Mohawk,* a
Cherokee, and what not *.

A word more, and I have done. You have been
pleafed to exprefs fome reluctance at fpreading what

* Surely this inftance of the *Monthly* Reviewer's partiality toward Mr. K. will fufficiently obviate the foolifh fufpicions of the
Candid Reviewers and others, of his being *himfelf* connected with
that work. What, becaufe a man may have been accidentally
obliged to take up his lodgings in a ftable, is he to be deemed an
horfe, or an oftler, for ever after? Misfortune may bring a man
acquainted, as Trinculo fays, with ftrange bed-fellows; but it is
his own fault if he does not change his companions with his circumftances.

you

you term *perfonalities*. There are many gentlemen
also, to whose judgment Mr. K. is ready to pay the
greatest deference, who express themselves, on the
present occasion, in the same strain. Nay, even some
of Dr. J's friends good-naturedly affect, like the
Monthly Reviewers, to think Mr. K. hath forgot
" the respect due to his own rank in the republick of
" letters," by descending, as they call it, to *such perfonalities*. But, if they say this of the author of the
Review of Dr. J's Shakespeare, what will they say of
the author of this *Defence* of it?—Doubtless, ten times
worse; but I care not.—As to all those, who are
justly reprehended in this pamphlet, they will of course
exclaim loudly against my having exposed the petty
particulars of their pitiful and disingenuous conduct
with regard to Mr. K. and his writings. They will
naturally cry it down as *low*, as *illiberal*, and so forth.
It is not for the interest of *offenders* that their actions
should be too *minutely* scrutinized; they must unani-
mously plead for the use of *general* reflections only, in
order that the accusation may, " like a wild-goose,
" fly, unclaimed of any man;" but the justice due to
the individual *person* injured, claims a like peculiar re-
taliation of *personalities*. It were a degradation, indeed,
of any man's character to become a common thief-
taker or informer; but it can be none for him to seize
or prosecute those, who may have meanly picked his
own pocket, or basely attempted to assassinate his
friend. It would redound, in like manner, little to
the honour of a man of rank or fortune, to stoop so
low as to go to boxing with a Slack or a Broughton;

but,

3

but, perhaps, the firſt nobleman in the kingdom would not be diſpleaſed to poſſeſs their athletic abilities: in which caſe, I apprehend, the world would think it no impeachment of his dignity, if, highly provoked, he ſhould for once wave his privilege, and chaſtiſe the offender, of what rank ſo ever, at his own weapons. And thus, even ſuppoſing Mr. K's enthuſiaſtic plea of *juſtifying the dead* ſhould, in the more prudential opinion of the *living*, be condemned as chimerical; he hath, at *worſt*, only indulged his *paſſons* at the expence of his *politeneſs*, and waved his pretenſions as " the *ſcholar* and the *gentleman*," to *expoſe* his abilities as a MAN, *gentle* or *ſimple*, as the reader may determine.

In the mean time, nothing could be more unbecoming Mr. K. than, through meanneſs or affectation, to ſue for that determination in his favour, which the publick, without knowing it, have, in a great degree, already made. For, however *unneceſſarily particular* I may be thought to have been in the foregoing ſheets, the publick are yet to learn the principal motives of that confidence, which Mr. K. ſeems, on their ſuffrage, to have aſſumed.

The *Reviewer of Dr. Johnſon's Shakeſpeare*, indeed, hath too long and too ſucceſsfully laboured in the literary vineyard *, to need *now*, by any ſervile or ſiniſter means, to ſolicit his reward. No: the ſmall portion

---

* *Like a* MOLE, ſays the ingenious and ſarcaſtical author of the *Traveller*. This troglodite, however, hath now made his appearance above ground; and poſſibly Mr. G. (as well as Dr. J.) wiſhes he had remained working like a *mole* ſtill.

of

of literary fame, to which Mr. K. hath at any time made, or hereafter may make, pretenfions, he claims, with proper deference to the publick, not as a *favour*, but as his *due*. He thinks it not lefs difgraceful to *beg* of the multitude than of an individual ; and as he would not willingly *give* undeferved applaufe to *others*, he fcorns to *accept* it *himfelf*. His demands are few, and his expectations *moderate* ; but, fuch as they are, he hath fufficient reafon to think they will be complied with ; for, in fpite of artifice and cabal †, fooner or later, the PUBLICK *will be* JUST.

R. R.

† Yet to fo great a height is this fpirit of caballing carried ; that, if a fpeedy check be not put to it, the publick muft foon be content with fuch entertainment as is catered for them by a junto of opulent printers and bookfellers. The reader will hardly believe it poffible, yet fo it is, that I applied myfelf, with regard to the prefent performance, to near half a dozen different publifhers, before I could find one who would venture to fell a pamphlet, *reflecting*, as they faid, on the refpectable and tremendous compilers and printers of the *Reviews*, *Magazines*, and *Evening Chronicles*. Such is the prefent ftate of literature ! in which, it is in vain that the *liberty of the prefs* is fecured by law, when the publication of what is printed (and even the printing what is written, unlefs a man hath a prefs of his own) may be prevented by the combinations of printers and bookfellers.

F I N S.